LONDON – VEG...

There are over 100 vegetarian restaurants in London.
30 are inside the Circle Line. But you'll never find most of them
without this guide.

Vegetarian London features:

120 veggie restaurants across the capital.
15 restaurants within 10 minutes walk of Oxford Street.
23 all-you-can-eat veggie buffets for £6 or less.
Detailed reviews with prices, hours, sample dishes,
plus what's on the menu for vegans.
50 more ethnic restaurants with big veggie menus.
Every single health food and wholefood store.
Maps, features on vegetarian living, local veggie groups.

New in this edition:

160 extra pages – biggest guide ever!
Veggie munchie maps of the West End, City, Marylebone,
Covent Garden, Bloomsbury, Islington and Vegetarian
Republic of Stoke Newington.
30 fabulous new vegetarian restaurants and cafes.
Bursting with yummy veggie goodness!

Over 25,000 copies sold !

Praise for previous editions of Vegetarian London

"For people living in or visiting the capital, this book is more important than the A–Z." – **The Vegetarian Society**

"A thorough run down of health and food shops, restaurants serving vegetarian food, green shops and places to buy cruelty-free cosmetics and clothes." – **Time Out**

"You'll have no trouble finding nosh with this remarkably thorough guide to everything vegetarian in London."
– **Tony Banks MP**

"From Wood Green to Wimbledon, the book is a comprehensive catalogue of the best restaurants, shops and tourist attractions in the capital." – **The Big Issue**

"The most striking thing about this hand-sized guide to all things animal friendly is its appeal to non-vegetarians." – **The Big Issue**

"This well laid out guide ... tells you where to buy cruelty-free cosmetics, leather-free clothing and even lists dozens of organisations where you can meet people who want to enjoy a fun lifestyle that is not at the expense of animals." – **Traveller Magazine**

"A feast of food for under six pounds." – **BBC Vegetarian Good Food**

Vegetarian
London

By Alex Bourke and Jennifer Wharton

400 places to eat and shop

published by
Vegetarian Guides

VEGETARIAN LONDON (4th edition)
By Alex Bourke & Jennifer Wharton

ISBN 1-902259-033
This edition published January 2002,
reprinted with updates April 2003, by Vegetarian Guides Ltd,
PO Box 2284, London W1A 5UH, England.
www.vegetarianguides.com   info@vegetarianguides.com
Fax (+44) (0) 870-121 4721
First published in June 1994 as the Cruelty-Free Guide to London

UK, Ireland and Worldwide distribution: Portfolio Books
Unit 5, Perivale Industrial Park, Horsenden Lane South,
Greenford, Middlesex UB6 7RL, England.
Tel: (+44) 020-8997 9000, Fax: (+44) 020-8997 9097
sales@portfoliobooks.com
Also available from Gardners, Bertrams,
Suma, Marigold, Infinity

USA and Canada book trade distributor: Casemate
2114 Darby Road, Havertown, PA 19083, USA
Tel: 610-853 9131, Fax: 610-853 9146
casemate@casematepublishing.com

Vegetarian Guides available worldwide mail order at
www.vegetarianguides.com

Printed and bound in Great Britain by
Ebenezer Baylis, Worcester

Credits

Photos by Lisa Holgersson, Mike Bourke, Mickaël Charbonnel, Jennifer Wharton.
Cover design, layout and maps by Mickaël Charbonnel
Cover photo by Lisa Holgersson
Vegetarian Guides logo design: Marion Gillet
Veggie Cover Boys: Mickaël Charbonnel, Sam Pullen, Matt Parkinson

Contributors: Vanessa Clarke, Peter Despard, Paul Gaynor, Marion Gillet, Dr Michael Grill, Katrina Holland, Brian Jacobs, Christine Klein, Läyne Kuirk-Schwarz-Waad, Laurence Klein, Sue Lee, Peter Mason, Sherry Nicholls, everyone at London Vegans, Julie Rosenfield, Bani Sethi, Zofia Torun, Ania Truszkowska, Ronny Worsey and everyone else ... THANK YOU!!

Also published by Vegetarian Guides:

- *Vegetarian Britain*, 700 places to eat and sleep
- *Vegetarian France*, 150 places to eat and sleep
- *Vegetarian Europe*, 300 places to eat in Europe's top destinations

For more veggie travel guides and updates to this book visit

www.vegetarianguides.com

About Veggie Guides

Alex Bourke gave up a career as a software engineer to set up Vegetarian Guides to map the world for vegetarians and vegans. His aim was to make it easy to eat cruelty free anywhere in the world. Since 1991 he's travelled widely on four continents, working with the world's leading veggie and vegan activists and creating an unrivalled research network. As well as publishing our own guides, Vegetarian Guides buys in great veggie travel guides from other publishers to sell mail order and can provide info on eating pretty much anywhere in the world. We just haven't gotten around to writing it all down yet. That's where we hope you'll come in.

We don't do the usual naff reviews by a person who's tasted one dish at 1,000 restaurants in 3 months. Instead we list all the nice looking vegan dishes with prices, and get as much info as we can from local veggies who eat there all the time. We don't judge. If a place isn't up to standard we leave it out. We figure if it's still open someone likes it, so we give enough info for the students to pick the cheapie places, the couples to spot the ones with candles, and the business types to know where to go to impress. Of course if a place delights everyone we might rave about it.

Vegetarianism is growing explosively. Veganism is growing even faster within vegetarianism. The veggie market is bigger than the gay market, yet hardly addressed at all by the media and travel guides beyond a few token listings. We are building the first truly comprehensive series of guides, in partnership with the people best placed to write them, the coordinators of local and national vegetarian organisations in each country.

We are doing for veggies what Lonely Planet, Rough Guides, Let's Go and Moon have done for independent travellers, making full use of the opportunities provided by the internet, cheap international phone calls and travel.

When there's a veggie guide to every city and country, it will be easy for everyone in the world to eat veggie, and we will retire.

If you'd like to help us to map the rest of the world and fill in the gaps, write (or publish – we'll tell you how) a guide for your town or a section of one of our guides, or you have some suggestions or recommendations, we'd love to hear from you.

Happy travels!

www.vegetarianguides.co.uk, info@vegetarianguides.co.uk
Vegetarian Guides Ltd, PO Box 2284, London W1A 5UH, UK

VEGETARIAN TRAVELLERS' CHECKS

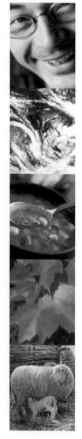

Every week we help hundreds of our members with their travel plans, offering them advice on where to stay and where to eat both at home and abroad.

Our members are also entitled to discounts at over 800 establishments worldwide and their exclusive hotline provides useful translations and phrases and lists of guest houses, restaurants and health food stores.

Our activities range from major promotions such as National Vegetarian Week to working with the food and catering industry, health professionals, caterers and school children. We also teach the best of vegetarian cookery at our **Cordon Vert Cookery School** in the heart of Cheshire.

We are an independent voice when it comes to issues such as BSE and vegetarian nutrition. To let that voice be heard we need your support.

For a free starter pack and membership details call today on 0161 925 2000 or email your request to info@vegsoc.org

Vegetarian
SOCIETY

Parkdale Dunham Road Altrincham
Cheshire WA14 4QG
Tel: 0161 925 2000 email: info@vegsoc.org
www.vegsoc.org

REGISTERED CHARITY NO. 259358

Vegetarian London
Table of contents

Maps

Introduction
Vegetarian Heaven

Alex Bourke, co-author of Vegetarian London since 1994, reveals an explosion of demand for vegetarian food in London and assesses the trends in eating out, ethnic dining and desserts.

In 1945 there were 100,000 vegetarians in Britain, all considered eccentric. By 1975 we were one million. Cranks restaurants served thick crust pasties and macrobiotic eateries required you to chew every worthy mouthful thirty times. At least that's how the world perceived us. As 1984 dawned, vegetarianism's most popular advocate was windy hippy Neil in *The Young Ones*.

Just as we seemed doomed to lentil jokes for eternity, Linda McCartney and a funky new Vegetarian Society laid the bearded, beaded, spaced out New Age stereotype to rest. Suddenly we were cool and veggie celebs 'came out' in droves. Pizza, pasta and salad bars took over the high street. The veggie-lution stormed on through the nineties until today there are over four million of us. According to the Vegetarian Society, 250,000 take the plunge each year, but a new survey reveals that a hundred times as many are veggie at least two days a week. Now that I've got your attention, let's look at how and why.

British meat eaters consume a third less than the French and half as much as Americans. A survey in summer 2000 for the RSPCA revealed that only 38% of meat eaters eat it daily, 21% four or five times a week, 33% two or three times and 8% just once a week or less. In other words, an incredible 60% of people have become demi-vegetarian, a trend that is tremendously benefiting the best veggie restaurants. Country Life vegan restaurant near Piccadilly surveyed their lunchtime customers and found that 70% are omnivores, proving that vegetarian is as much a mainstream cuisine in its own right as Indian.

Some vegetarian restaurants have been going out of business as customers drift off to non-veggie places that have started to copy veggie dishes. With even Burger King and McDonald's doing veggieburgers, is there still enough demand for vegetarian restaurants to survive in the ubiquiveg noughties? Oh yes, but only if they stay on the innovative leading edge.

Compiling the last four editions of *Vegetarian London*, it's clear that traditional cheese and egg *cooking* is losing ground to grain and bean based *world cuisine*. In ten years veggiedom expanded steadily from three to four million, but vegans have surged meteorically from 80,000 in 1993 to a quarter of a million in 2000 (RealEat survey). Every fourth group of four veggie diners now includes a vegan. Many veggies too are fed up to the back teeth with cheese toppings on every dish and are going for vegan food in droves. Far from limiting your choices by removing cheese and eggs, eating modern international vegan opens up the richest and most diverse cuisine of all, with hundreds of new ingredients, a riotously colourful, multi-textured, aromatic, herby-spicy, melt in your mouth fusion of African, south-east Asian, Japanese, Indian and middle Eastern dishes plus heaps of raw and steamed veg. The invention of vegan chocolate cake, apple pie, soya cream, ice-cream and custard means no more fuming over a boring sorbet or fruit salad while your mates tuck into something sinful. We've nobly tried them all and in this guide we tell you where they are.

If you want a taste of the future, here are some legendary vegetarian restaurants that attract regulars from all over London, setting the trail with ethnic and new vegan cuisine of quite astonishing breadth and deliciousness. **The Gate** in Hammersmith or Hampstead, and **Manna** by Primrose Hill, are great for a de luxe, romantic dinner à deux with big menus and charming service. They have recently been joined by **Plant** in the West End. Diners flock from across the south to **Riverside Vegetaria** in Kingston-upon-Thames with its beautiful setting, eleven vegan main courses and seventeen desserts. London has ten yummy new Chinese vegan restaurants, including **Tai** in Greek Street and **Peking Palace** in Holloway. For a bargain lunch or midnight refuelling, visit the new vegetarian falafel cafe **Maoz** in Old Compton Street.

Getting away is no longer a problem for us. Every month brings a new addition to the UK's eighty vegetarian guesthouses, many competing to serve the biggest and most extensive cooked breakfast. The most satisfying in Britain has to be Hugh Wilson and Suzanne Allen's Edinburgh **Greenhouse Guesthouse**, featuring rashers, sausages, mushrooms, baked beans, hashbrowns, tomatoes, scrambled tofu, bagels with Tofutti cream cheese, croissants, brioches, pancakes with maple syrup, juices, cereals, fruit salad and vegan yoghurt. For further gourmet getaways, see our Travel section at the end of this guide, try a *Vegi Ventures* holiday, or if you're from out of town then spend a few days in one of London's vegetarian hotels and guest houses listed under Accommodation.

The number of veggies in Britain has increased forty fold in 55 years. Despite massive subsidies, the meat and dairy industries continue to decline and indeed pork, lamb and beef would collapse without state intervention. Whereas without any support, our kind of food is showing strong growth both in restaurants and retailers. This is just the beginning. One day I expect to see a vegetarian restaurant on every street, as in India. The future has never looked brighter, healthier, or more profitable for London's one million vegetarians, 150 health and wholefood stores, 120 vegetarian restaurants, and the thousands of shops, supermarkets and eateries that have been extending their vegetarian range. Vegetarianism, and especially veganism, really are the food of the future, and we will continue to direct you to the very best there is in the vegetarian paradise that is London.

Alex Bourke is a director of the Vegan Society and founder of Vegetarian Guides. He roams the world writing, speaking and broad-casting on vegan issues and vegetarian travel. Books he has co-authored include Vegetarian London, Vegetarian France, Vegetarian Britain, Vegetarian Europe *and* Campaign Against Cruelty – an activist's handbook. *All these guides are available from bookshops or mail order from Vegetarian Guides Ltd, PO Box 2284, London W1A 5UH. Website www.vegetarianguides.com*

New in this edition

This fourth edition has 100 extra pages – our biggest guide ever! We've added veggie munchie maps of the West End, Covent Garden, Bloomsbury, Marylebone & Fitzrovia, City, Islington and Vegetarian Republic of Stoke Newington. There are at least 30 fabulous new vegetarian restaurants. This book is bursting with yummy veggie goodness and here are some of the highlights.

Five years ago you could count London's vegan restaurants on one hand. Now you need to take your shoes off. Reflecting the trend in the veggie world away from eggs and dairy, vegan restaurants have mushroomed in the capital.

Entrepreneurs from a Buddhist temple have started up no less than ten new vegetarian Chinese restaurants with charming staff and an amazing vegan buffet that you can visit as many times as you like for £5–£6. If you order Chinese tea you get unlimited refills. Find them at:
Tai, 10 Greek Street, West End
Chi, 55 St Martins Lane, Covent Garden
Joi, 14 Percy Street, off Tottenham Court Rd
CTJ, 339 Euston Road, Fitzrovia
CTB, 88 Leather Lane, The City
SASA, 13 Islington High Street, Islington
CTV, 22 Golders Green Road, North London
SASA, 271 Muswell Hill Broadway, North London
Kai, 244 West Hendon Broadway, North West London
Chai, 236 Station Road, Edgware, North West London
Vegan Thai Buffet, 167 The Vale, Acton, West End

Other new Oriental vegetarian restaurants are:
Peking Palace, 669 Holloway Road, North London
VitaOrganic, 279c Finchley Road, North West London
Sayur Mayur, 87 Battersea Rise, Clapham
Veggie One, 322 Limpsfield Rd, South Croydon, Surrey

For fast food, grab a falafel at
Maoz, *47 Old Compton Street, West End;*
a falafel or veggie burger at
Red Veg, *95 Dean Street, West End;*
and sandwiches, wraps, soup or a salad at
Plant, *47 Poland Street, West End,* which has now added a gourmet vegetarian restaurant behind the cafe; and finally
JJ's Wrap Kitchen, *Citypoint, 1 Ropemaker Street, The City.*

These terrific new places help to fill the gaps left by **Cranks**, whose owners ploughed millions into revamping their high rent locations in the nineties without doing enough to update the food. Or rather they hired a food consultant who wasn't even a veggie with predictable results. In 2001 they finally caught on that more vegan dishes and clear labelling of ingredients is essential these days. Turnover began to rise, but not fast enough to convince their venture capitalist non-veggie masters and alas all five London branches closed. It's a tragedy that such a lovely chain of cafés went down because the people at the top were out of touch with what is going on in the veggie world, as in how can you really understand what we want if you're not one of us?

Crazy Salads was a new chain of veggie salad bars that flourished post-Cranks, then was sold off in 2002 to new owners. They increased prices 25% and introduced meat and cheesey toppings. Takings fell three-quarters. The moral of both stories is don't put a meat eater in charge of a vegetarian restaurant unless you have very deep pockets and like learning the hard way.

Fortunately there are plenty of new vegetarian restaurants run by veggies who are getting it right:
Blue Ginger, *Barnet, North London*
Chawalla, *Forest Gate, East London*
The Gate 2, *72 Belsize Lane, North West London*
Indigo, *Park Royal, West London*
Jashan, *1-2 Coronet Parade, Ealing Road, Middlesex*
Mangoes, *191 Hartfield Rd, Wimbledon, South London*
Pradip, *154 Kenton Rd, Harrow, Middlesex*
Ram's Gujarati Surti Cuisine, *203 Kenton Road, Harrow, Middx*
Sagar, *157 King St, Hammersmith, West London*
Vegetarian Paradise, *59 Marchmont St, Bloomsbury*

New veggie cafés:

Brothers Green, *Chelsea, Sloane Zone*
Coopers, *17 Lower Marsh, Waterloo, South London*
Domali, *38 Westow St, Crystal Palace, South London*
Fresh & Wild, *Brewer Street, West End*
Planet Organic, *22 Torrington Place, Bloomsbury*
Queens Wood Cafe, *Highgate Wood, North London*
St Paul's Vegetarian Café, *1 St Paul's Rd, Islington*
Tony's Natural Foods, *10 Caledonian Road, Islington*
Yogi Ji's, *658 Kingsbury Rd, North West London*

London now has its first raw food centre, **We Are Raw (W.A.R.)** in North London. Just as veganism is the leading edge of vegetarianism, so for many raw food is the leading edge of veganism. Would you believe that you can make raw food cakes and biscuits, for example, that taste just like the "real thing" but are actually healthier? Come and be amazed.

There are many new wholefood and health food stores since the last edition. **GNC** have been taking over or opening new shops, but the biggest splash has been made by wholefood organic supermarket **Fresh and Wild**, now up to six branches in Soho, Camden, The City, Westbourne Grove, Stoke Newington and Lavender Hill. Like the two branches of **Planet Organic** in Westbourne Grove and Bloomsbury, they feature a staggering range of vegan and vegetarian organic foods, toiletries and cosmetics, juice bars, deli and sometimes a café, and have well trained staff and consultants to answer all your questions. And they're open late night and Sundays.

What to do late at night when the veggie restaurant is closed? We've included a few omnivorous restaurants with big veggie menus where we recognised that many vegetarians eat there, either through choice, or when in a big group of friends who don't want to go where we do. Top of the list of handy places for when your mates veto a veggie venue is Japanese fast food noodle restaurant **Wagamama**, now up to 10 branches in London offering at least 9 veggie or vegan dishes. Find them in Bloomsbury, Covent Garden, Marylebone, West End, Sloane Zone, Kensington (West), Camden and Kingston (Surrey).

boycott
IAMS

10 out of 10 cats & dogs prefer not to suffer in cruel IAMS experiments

SUNDAY EXPRESS

PET FOOD CRUELTY EXPOSED

Cats and dogs suffered in experiments for top brand

Uncaged Campaigns uncovered 24 scientific papers that describe how IAMS funded laboratory experiments on 460 healthy animals that caused kidney failure, obesity, malnutrition, liver damage, stomach inflammation, lesions.....many animals died or were killed.

Join the IAMS and Eukanuba boycott

For more information contact: Uncaged Campaigns
St. Mattew's House, 45 Carver Street, Sheffield S1 4FT
Tel: 0114 272 2220   Web: www.uncaged.co.uk

Introduction
Jen's guide to coffee houses

Don't panic if you can't find a veggie outlet to hand, some of the high street names do a few veggie and vegan options for those on the move. Here are just three of the biggest chains.

PRET A MANGER

Several veggie sandwiches and a really tasty houmous and pepper one which is quite filling. They have cartons of salads and fresh fruit salads to take away, even veggie crisps and sushi. Food is always clearly labelled and is guaranteed to be very freshly prepared, though you'll pay a bit more than elsewhere.

STARBUCKS

The first large coffee house to cater for coffee loving vegans by always having soya milk for great soyaccinos and soya lattes. The branch in Borders bookshop at the top of Charing Cross Road has floppy armchairs where you can read books for free. Bizarrely Starbucks started putting skimmed milk in the bread for otherwise vegan hummous sandwiches then stopped doing sandwiches altogether. Coffee Republic may also do soya milk on request.

BENJY'S

Basic, inexpensive take-away food with several veggie sandwich options and at least two vegan ones. Unfortunately they don't list their ingredients so it's difficult to figure out what is truly veggie or vegan. They say clear labelling is planned for the future.

Vegetarian London
How to use this guide

We've arranged this guide by area, so that wherever you are, you'll find all the shops and restaurants together.

The core of the book is the **West End** (restaurants, theatres, cinemas and night life), **Bloomsbury** (British Museum), **Covent Garden** (natty boutiques make browsing heaven), **Marylebone and Fitzrovia** (north side of Oxford Street) and **The City** (sightseeing and making millions). For each area we've included a map with all our recommended restaurants, cafes and shops to help you plan your scoffing tour of London.

This is followed by the **Sloane Zone** (Knightsbridge and Chelsea, yah), **Islington** where everyone ends up at some point, and **Stoke Newington** which has many fine eateries and perhaps the densest concentration of veggies in London. The listings round off with **Camden**, where the huge market is definitely worth a Saturday or Sunday, and comprehensive sections for **North London, North West, East End, West London, Waterloo, Brixton & Clapham, South London, Middlesex and Surrey.**

We've added **tabs** down the sides of the pages to help you locate areas quickly, and there are lots of **indexes** at the end of the book plus additional ones at the start of each section.

At the end of the guide is a quick list of **ethnic restaurants** and an expanded **accommodation** section, now listing central hostels, ideal for backpackers who don't want to eat out twice a day. There are **caterers** for veggie weddings and parties, vegan chef **Ronny's Top Tips** for keen cooks, a new guide to cruelty free shopping for **cosmetics and toiletries**, a directory of **local groups** where residents and tourists alike can make new friends or get active, and an expanded **Getting Away** section full of ideas for romantic and fun weekends out of London.

Name of the place

Type of place

Chapter finder

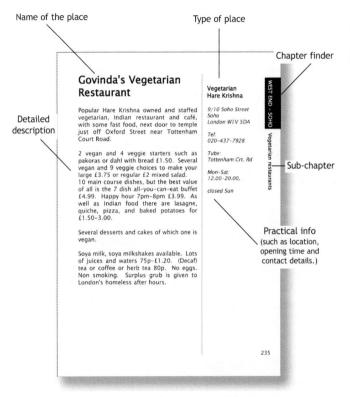

Govinda's Vegetarian Restaurant

Detailed description

Popular Hare Krishna owned and staffed vegetarian, Indian restaurant and café, with some fast food, next door to temple just off Oxford Street near Tottenham Court Road.

2 vegan and 4 veggie starters such as pakoras or dahl with bread £1.50. Several vegan and 9 veggie choices to make your large £3.75 or regular £2 mixed salad. 10 main course dishes, but the best value of all is the 7 dish all-you-can-eat buffet £4.99. Happy hour 7pm–8pm £3.99. As well as Indian food there are lasagne, quiche, pizza, and baked potatoes for £1.50–3.00.

Several desserts and cakes of which one is vegan.

Soya milk, soya milkshakes available. Lots of juices and waters 75p–£1.20. (Decaf) tea or coffee or herb tea 80p. No eggs. Non smoking. Surplus grub is given to London's homeless after hours.

Vegetarian
Hare Krishna

9/10 Soho Street
Soho
London W1V 5DA

Tel:
020–437–7928

Tube:
Tottenham Crt. Rd

Mon–Sat:
12.00–20.00,

closed Sun

WEST END – SOHO

Vegetarian restaurants

Sub-chapter

Practical info
(such as location, opening time and contact details.)

235

23

24

Central London
West End – Soho

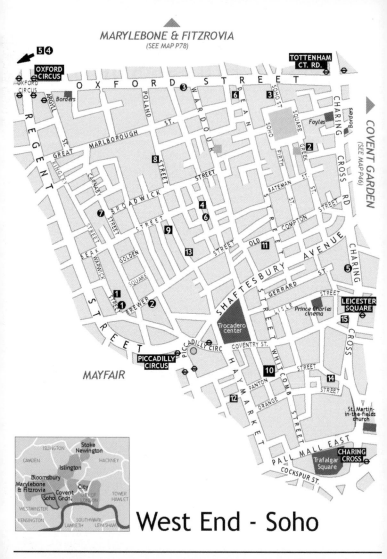

MARYLEBONE & FITZROVIA
(SEE MAP P78)

TOTTENHAM CT. RD.

OXFORD CIRCUS

OXFORD STREET

COVENT GARDEN
(SEE MAP P46)

Borders

Foyles

POLAND ST.

DEAN STREET

WARDOUR STREET

SOHO SQUARE

GREEK ST.

FRITH ST.

CHARING CROSS RD.

MARLBOROUGH

GREAT MARLBOROUGH

KING'S

ARGYLL ST.

BROADWICK STREET

CARNABY STREET

BEAK STREET

WARWICK STREET

GOLDEN SQUARE

BREWER STREET

BATEMAN ST.

OLD COMPTON STREET

GERRARD STREET

LISLE STREET

SHAFTESBURY AVENUE

WARDOUR STREET

DEAN STREET

FRITH STREET

GREEK STREET

CHARING CROSS RD.

CHARING CROSS RD.

LEICESTER SQUARE

Prince Charles cinema

Trocadero center

PICCADILLY CIRCUS

COVENTRY ST.

HAYMARKET

WHITCOMB STREET

PANTON STREET

ORANGE STREET

St. Martin-in-the-fields church

MAYFAIR

PALL MALL EAST

CHARING CROSS

Trafalgar Square

COCKSPUR ST.

ISLINGTON

Stoke Newington

CAMDEN

HACKNEY

Islington

Bloomsbury

Marylebone & Fitzrovia

Covent Grdn.

CITY OF LONDON

TOWER HAMLET

Soho

WESTMINSTER

KENSINGTON

SOUTHWARK

LAMBETH

LEWISHAM

West End - Soho

Places in the West End

■ Vegetarian restaurants

■ Omnivorous restaurants

● Wholefood & health food shops

Central London's healthiest restaurant, near Piccadilly

Country Life

Vegan restaurant

Herbivore heaven at this central vegan wholefood restaurant, mainly organic.

Brilliant buffet all-you-can-eat lunch of mixed salads and hot dishes which you pay for by weight, maximum £5.95 for a plate.

No longer open in the evenings except for Thursday, when the buffet is £7 and there is also gourmet à la carte. Soup from £2.20, starters from £2.25, main course from £7.95. Mains include Tofu Rissoles made with organic tofu, bulgar, fresh onion puree, olive oil, parsely, garlic powder and oregano; Mediterranean Courgette with organic butter beans, tomato sauce, fresh onions and basil.

Desserts from £2 are all vegan (but you'd never know!) such as Viennese apple strudel, Tofutti vanilla ice cream, blackberry terrine, tofu cheese cake.

Alcohol free wine and other non alcoholic drinks. Smoke free. Booking advised in the evening. On Fridays restaurant closes 15.30 summer, 14.30 winter.

Wholefood shop upstairs with vegan yogurt and ice-cream, cookbooks, wholemeal bread and rolls, biscuits and snacks. Shop open Mon–Thu 9–18.00, Fri till 15.30, Sun 13.00–17.00.

Their resident vegan GP is available for private consultations.

3–4 Warwick Street near Piccadilly London W1

Tel:
020-7434 2922

Tube:
Piccadilly Circus exit 1

Sun–Fri:
11.30–16.00 (last orders),

also Thur eve: 18.00–22.30

Closed Sat.

Tai Vegan Restaurant

Organic vegan Chinese. London's newest veggie restaurant, run by a Buddhist temple, and already incredibly popular for its amazing value and delicious food. Mainly Chinese and Thai food, some Japanese.

All you can eat buffet, as many trips as you like for £5, or £6 in the evenings, £3 for a take-away box. Rice, spring rolls, tofu, stir-fry veg, salad, soya meats, noodles, menu changes all the time.

All vegetables are organic and the soya is GM free. Tea £1, all organic juices £2.50, soft drinks such as natural cola £1.

Cash only. Non-smoking.

Vegan Chinese Restaurant

10 Greek Street
Soho
London W1V 5PL

Tel:
020-7287 3730

Tube:
Tottenham Court Rd,
Leicester Sq

Mon-Sat:
12.30–21.30,

Sun:
13–21.00

Govinda's Vegetarian Restaurant

Vegetarian
Hare Krishna

Popular Hare Krishna owned and staffed vegetarian, Indian restaurant and café, with some fast food, next door to their temple, just off Oxford Street and near Tottenham Court Road.

9/10 Soho Street
Soho
London W1V 5DA

2 vegan and 4 veggie starters such as pakoras or dahl with bread £1.50. Several vegan and 9 veggie choices to make your large £3.75 or regular £2 mixed salad.

Tel:
020-7437-7928

10 main course dishes, but the best value of all is the 7 dish all-you-can-eat buffet £4.99. Happy hour 7pm-8pm £3.99. As well as Indian food there are pizza and baked potatoes for £1.50-3.00.

Tube:
Tottenham Court Rd

Mon-Sat:
12.00-20.00,

Several desserts and cakes of which one is vegan.

closed Sun

Soya milk, soya milkshakes available. Lots of juices and waters 75p-£1.20. (Decaf) tea or coffee or herb tea 80p. No eggs. Non smoking. Surplus grub is given to London's homeless after hours.

Beatroot, the best vegan cake selection in the West End

Beatroot

Our favourite central London café, with almost all desserts now vegan, near the south end of Berwick St by the fruit and veg market.

Point to whatever you fancy from 16 hot dishes and salads and they'll fill a box for you, small £2.90, medium £3.90 or large £4.90. Choose from, for example, tomato walnut and spinach pasta, spicy Moroccan tangine, ratatouille, brown rice, all kinds of salads. Soup with bread £2.40.

Lots of cakes, mostly vegan, £1–£2.40 including fabulous vegan chocolate dream cake, with vegan custard 40p extra, vegan tofu cheesecake, carrot cake, hemp flapjacks, and rum and walnut balls.

Fresh organic juices like Vitalizer (apple, carrot, ginger), Beatnik (beatroot, carrot, celery) or Vego (celery, spinach, carrot), 9oz for £2.20 or 12oz for £2.90. "Booster" health drink (banana, spirulina and peanut butter) £1.90 or £2.40. Gorgeous soya–fruit smoothies made with raspberry, mango or blueberry, small £1.40, large £1.90. Teas 90p, filter coffee £1.

They do take–away and sandwiches too so it gets a bit manic at lunchtime, whereas in the afternoon you could sit quietly here and write a letter. Couple of outside tables. Smoking allowed outside. No credit cards.

Veggie & Vegan cafe

*92 Berwick Street
Soho
London W1V 3PP*

*Tel:
020 7437 8591*

*Tube:
Oxford Circus,
Tottenham Crt. Rd.*

*Mon–Sat:
9.00 –18.15*

Call them to be faxed the latest menu. They can prepare orders in advance for 5 or more people.

Rasa W1 in Dering Street

Top class, subtle Keralan cuisine

Rasa W1

South Indian restaurant on two floors, specialising in Keralan cuisine, vegetarian downstairs, omnivorous upstairs.

Take-away Rasa Express lunches £2.50 like veg biriyiana, mini masala dosa, wrap filled with mixed veg, or a mixture.

A la carte pre meal snacks £4 include nibbles made from root vegetables, rice, coconut milk, flour, lentils and seeds all beautifully spiced. 10 starters, £4.25, include cassava root steamed with tumeric, curry leaves and green chillies; fried plantain in rice and chickpea batter with peanut and ginger sauce. Soups £4.50.

Three types of dosas £10.95. 50 curry dishes £6.25, including exotic ingredients such as sweet mangoes, green banana, breadfruit, tamarind, bottle gourd, coconut and other Keralan delicacies.

6 side dishes at £5.25 such as shredded green papaya with fresh coconut and green chillies served with spiced dhal and mustard seeds. 7 kinds of rice £3–£3.75.

Several desserts include banana dosa (vegan) £3.50, mango sorbet £2.75

Wine from £9.50 bottle, £2.50 glass. Champagne £24.95 or £31.95. Beers £2.75. Soft drinks £1.50.

Vegetarian
South Indian

6 Dering Street
off Oxford Street
London W1

Tel:
020-7629 1346

Tube: Oxford Circus

Mon–Sat:
12.00–15.00 &
18–23.00.

Sun:
18–23.00

12% optional service
charge

No smoking

Reservations
recommended

WEST END – SOHO   Vegetarian restaurants

Maoz

Falafel cafe

Fantastic new falafel bar like the ones in Amsterdam, at the west end of the gay zone, specialising in falafel in pitta, £2.50–£3.50. Self serve salad bar with large choice of salads and tahini which you pile on top of your falafel, all of which are vegan apart from the coleslaw and mayonnaise. Eat in or take-away. Non smoking. No credit cards.

*43 Old Compton St
Soho
London W1*

Tel: 020–7851 1586

Tube: Leicester Square

*Mon–Fri:
11.00am–02.00am
later at weekends*

www.maozfalafel.nl

Red Veg

Veggie & vegan take-away

London's first veggie burger and falafel bar with a few tables, just off Oxford Street in the next street west of Soho Square. The whole menu is GM free and from independently created recipes.

Veggie burger £2.65, can be made spicy with kidney beans.. Chilli veg £2.65, Jamaican roll £2.65, Oriental noodles £2.95, falafel £2.95, noname nuggets £2.65.

Medium fries 75p, large 95p, plantain chips £1.15, crispy zucchini £1.15, breaded mushrooms £1.15.

Vietnamese style coffee, cappuccino, café latte, espresso, and tea all £1.00. Herbal teas £1.10.

*95 Dean Street,
Soho
London W1V 5RB*

Tel: 020–7437–3109

Tube: Tottenham Court Road

*Mon–Sat: til 22.00
Closed Sun*

Plant

New vegetarian **take-away and cafe** at the front with a few seats. Soups, lots of sandwiches such as vegan "cheddar", a salad bar and organic cakes. Smoothies, fresh juices, some organic juices, decaffeinated and specially blended coffee. Cooked veggie or vegan breakfasts.

Behind the cafe is a brand new gourmet **restaurant**. Starters are all vegan, £2.65-3.95, including pitta dips, marinated tofu crostini, Caribbean fried dumplings with hot chilli sauce, French onion soup or chef salad. Side orders, £1.25-2.75, such as garlic bread, rice, chunky chips, potatoes, chilli greens, salad, yam or plantain.

10 main courses (9 vegan), £7.95-11.50, such as tofu and veggie-mince burger with salad and fries; vegetable curry with coconut and tamarind sauce and turmeric fried rice; seitan stroganoff with herb cashew cream sauce; asparagus spelt pancakes; vegetarian meatballs with glazed vegetables and herb stock with rice or spaghetti; tofu or seitan stir-fry; wild mushroom risotto; marinated tofu Nicoise; East Meets West eastern and Afro-caribbean vegetables in spicy tomato and coriander sauce; or daily seasonal special.

Desserts, £3.25-3.70, include apple crumble with soya cream or ice-cream; spelt pancake with vanilla ice-cream topped with warm carob and vanilla sauce; fruit salad; organic cakes.

Vegetarian cafe and restaurant

47 Poland Street London W1F 7VB

Tel: 020-7734 7528 Fax: 020-7734 5984

Tube: Oxford Circus

Cafe: Mon–Thu 08.00–22.30, Fri 08.00–16.30

Restaurant: Mon–Thu 12.30–23.00, Fri 12.30–16.30, Sat 18.30–23.00

www. plantfooddrink.com info@ plantfooddrink.com

Not licensed

No smoking

Gluten and wheat free modifications usually available.

Catering and delivery for events. Directions: From Oxford Circus, go east along Oxford St. towards Tottenham Court Road. Turn right into Poland Street.

37

Mildreds

Stylish vegetarian café-restaurant and take-away with hip young clientele to match, crowded and enthusiastic. The food is modern European with some Asian influences.

Lunchtime specials £3.90 include burger of the day with fried or stir-fried veg with brown rice; bean falafel in tortilla with chilli sauce and tahini; energizing detox salad.

Lite bites like ciabata or walnut bread, veg spring rolls with chilli jam or tomato, red onion and basil salad, 70p to £3.75.

Many of the main courses are vegan, such as stir-fried veg in soy and sesame oil with ginger on organic brown rice for £5.30, add satay or chilli sauce £5.90, organic tofu £6.70; or Asian marinated mock duck for £6.30. There's also a larger detox salad with organic carrots, sprouted beans, chick peas, sultanas and toasted seeds with lemongrass and ginger dressing for £4.70, add miso soup for £7.00.

Several desserts include vegan double chocolate pudding with mocha sauce, or fruit crumble with soya cream, £2.20 to £3.30.

Fully licensed. Cheques but no cards. Optional 10% service charge added to the bill. No reservations but you can have a drink at the front while you wait.

45 Lexington Street
Soho
London W1

Tel:
020-7494 1634

Tube:
Piccadilly Circus,
Oxford Circus

Mon–Sat:
12–23.00,

Sun:
12.30–17.30

Woodlands Leicester Sq.

Vegetarian
South Indian

Vegetarian Indian restaurant off the south-west corner of Leicester Square, and one of three in London. Established for over 20 years in Britain, also the largest veggie chain of restaurants in India too, serving hungry customers since 1938.

This branch is open all day and offers a lunchtime all you can eat buffet on weekdays for £5.99 alongside their regular menu. For more details on the dishes please see the branch in Marylebone. (page 82)

37 Panton St
(off Haymarket)
London SW1Y 4EA

Tel:
020–7839 7258

Tube:
Piccadilly Circus,
Leicester Square

Every Day
12.00–23.00

Wagamama Haymarket

One of the newer branches of the omnivorous Japanese noodle chain and close by all the theatres.

For menus see Bloomsbury, WC1 branch.

www.wagamama.com

Omnivorous
Japanese fast food

8 Norris Street
off the Haymarket
London SW1Y 4RJ

Tel: 020–7321 2755

Tube: Leicester
Square

Mon–Sat:
12.00–23.00,

Sun: 12.30–22.30

Wagamama Lexington St.

Omnivorous fast food Japanese noodle bar with over nine veggie and vegan dishes. Very busy, totally authentic, heaps of fun.

Allow about £12–£15 for a belt-buster, less if your're only eating mains. Prices start at £1.25 for miso soup.

See Bloomsbury, WC1 branch for menu.

Omnivorous
Japanese fast food

10A Lexington Street
London W1R 3HS

Tel:
020–7292 0990

Tube:
Piccadilly Circus,
Oxford Circus

Mon–Sat:
12.00–Midnight,

Sun: 12.30–22.00.

Wagamama Leicester Sq.

**Omnivorous
Japanese fast food**

One of the many branches of this omnivorous fast food Japanese noodle bar with over nine veggie and vegan dishes. This one is just off Charing Cross Road, opposite the Garrick Theatre.

Allow about £10 or more for a starter and main course with drink. Prices start at £1.25 for a small miso soup up to £6.50 for an enormous bowl of miso ramen (noodles).

See Bloomsbury, WC1 branch for menu.

*14A Irving Street
West End
London WC1V*

*Tel:
020-7839 2323*

*Tube:
Leicester Square,
Charing Cross*

*Mon–Sat:
12.00–23.00, 24.00*

*Fri–Sat, Sun:
12.30–22.00*

Fresh & Wild

Huge organic wholefood supermarket on two floors in the middle of Brewer Street, with heaps of take-aways, a salad bar and juice bar/cafe with seating, organic fruit and vegetables, remedies and some books, including Veggie Guidess.

There's a great value self serve area right at the back upstairs where you can load up on grains, beans, nuts and dry fruit. This is where you'll also find Provamel soya desserts and at least six flavours of Swedish Glace vegan ice-cream.

Health food store & cafe / juice bar

75 Brewery Lane
Brewer Street
London W1R 3SL

Tel:
020-7434 3179

Tube: Piccadilly

Open:
late night and all weekend

Holland & Barrett

Fairly small branch of this national chain, but with large take-away section, and freezer counter.

Healthfoods store

123 Oxford St
London W1R 1TF

Tel:
020-7287 3624

Tube:
Oxford Circus,
Tottenham Court Rd

Mon-Wed:
8.30-18.45,

Thur-Fri:
8.30-19.45,

Sat: 10:00-18.45,
Sun: 12:00-16.45

Holland & Barrett

In the Bond St tube shopping complex, with a larger than usual selection of take-away savouries including sandwiches and vegan pasties and pies. Often have special offers on bulk buys of dried fruit and nuts.

Healthfoods store

Unit C12, West One Shopping Ctr

corner of Davis St. and Oxford St. by Bond Street underground

London W1R 1FE

Tel: 020–7493 7988

Tube: Bond Street

Holland & Barrett

Health food store just north of Leicester Square, great for flapjacks, dried fruit, nuts, vegan chocolate, drinks and snacks like pastries and pies.

Healthfoods store

65 Charing Cross Rd by Leicester Square London WC2H 0NE

Tel: 020–7287–3193

Tube: Leicester Sq.

Mon–Sat: 10.00–20.00, Sun: 11.00–18.00

43

Covent Garden

BLOOMSBURY
(SEE MAP P64)

TOTTENHAM
COURT RD.

OXFORD ST.

NEW OXFORD ST.

CHARING CROSS RD.

SAINT GILES HIGH ST.

2

SHAFTESBURY

AVENUE

ENDELL STREET

SHORTS GARDENS

NEAL ST.

6 1
5
4 3

10

NEAL ST.

SHELTON ST.

SHORTS GARDENS

EARLHAM STREET

BOW ST.

THE CITY
(SEE MAP P90) ▶

COVENT
GARDEN

Royal Opera
House ▼

CHARING CROSS

SAINT MARTIN'S LANE

LONG ACRE

FLORAL STREET

WELLINGTON ST.

COVENT GARDEN
THE MARKET
3

KING ST.

SOHO
(SEE MAP P26) ◀

LEICESTER
SQU.

8

GARRICK ST.

BEDFORD ST.

BEDFORDBURY

HENRIETTA ST.

MAIDEN LANE

7

1

CHANDOS PL.

CHARING CROSS RD.

ST. MARTIN'S

St. Martin's-
in-the-fields
church

ADELAIDE ST.

National
Gallery

TRAFALGAR
SQUARE

STRAND

VILLIERS ST.

CHARING
CROSS

2

VICTORIA
EMBKMT
GDNS

EMBANKMENT

SAVOY PLACE

VICTORIA EMBANKMENT

RIVER THAMES

PEDESTRIAN BRIDGE

ISLINGTON
CAMDEN
Stoke
Newington
HACKNEY
Islington
Bloomsbury
Marylebone
& Fitzrovia
Covent
Grdn
City
CITY OF
LONDON
TOWER
HAMLET
Soho
WESTMINSTER
KENSINGTON
SOUTHWARK
LAMBETH
LEWISHAM

Covent Garden

Places in Covent Garden

■ Vegetarian restaurants

■ Omnivorous restaurants

● Wholefood & health food shops

Chi

Chinese vegan
buffet restaurant

All you can eat Chinese vegan buffet restaurant, like the busier one in Greek Street (Soho), one block back from Charing Cross Road in the heart of theatreland.

Fill up at the West End's best value restaurant on fried and boiled rice, noodles, stir-fry vegetables, tofu, mushrooms and several kinds of fake meat, with as many visits to the buffet as you like for just £5 before 5.30pm, then £6 afterwards and all day Sunday.

Take-away £3.

55 St Martin's Lane
Covent Garden
London WC2

Tel: 020-7836 3434

Tube:
Leicester Square,
Charing Cross

Every day:
12.00-23.00
Sunday -22.00

First Out Coffee Shop

Vegetarian café and take-away

Smart, modern and very popular gay and lesbian vegetarian café with international menu and basement bar, close to Tottenham Court Road tube. Music for all tastes and low enough not to be intrusive. Can be lively or very laid back depending on time of day. 50 yards from Tottenham Court Road tube.

The soup of the day is always vegan for £2.95. Range of salad platters with dips and pitta bread for £4.50. On Sundays they do brunch.

For main course you could try the veg chilli or veg curry, pies, bakes, or nachos from £4.50 to £4.95.

Generally good for vegans until you get to the many cakes. Soya milk on request.

Glass of house white £2.95 to £3.95, £12–14.00 a bottle, beer £2.00 to £2.70. Smoking only in the bar downstairs. No credit cards.

They have party evenings and Friday night is 'Girl Friday' or women's night with men as guests.

52 St Giles High St
Covent Garden
London WC2H 8LH

Tel: 020-7240 8042

Tube:
Tottenham Ct. Rd.

Mon–Sat:
10.00–23.00,

Sun 11–22.30

Great veggie grub since 1974

Food For Thought

Vegan & veggie
restaurant

Extremely popular and successful veggie take-away and café on fascinating Neal Street in a vaulted basement. Pine tables and buzzy, cosmopolitan atmosphere. They offer good value and the food is very fresh with a global menu. It gets really crowded at peak times and you'll need to queue on the stairs at lunchtime for counter service. Many dishes are vegan or vegan option.

31 Neal Street
Covent Garden
London WC2H 9PR

Tel:
020-7836
9072/0239

Tube: Covent Garden

Mon-Sat:
12.00-20.30,

Sun: 12.00-17.00

The menu changes daily. Here are some examples: vegan carrot and butterbean soup or butternut squash soup £2.60; two bean salad, pasta with pesto, potato salad with tofu mayo all £3 to £5

Vegan main courses £3 to £6 include Ethiopian Wat; Middle Eastern mezze; Carri coco curry; Malay sambal; shepherdess pie; satay and tofu noodles; roast Mediterranean veg with polenta.

The evening menu from 5pm is slightly different, and might be cannelloni filled with aubergine, sundried tomatoes and basil served with polenta, broccoli and tomato frissée salad for £5.00 to £5.80.

Scrummy vegan desserts such as strawberry and vanilla scones, apple and plum crumble or fruit salad £2.80 to £3.10.

Lots of drinks including fresh juices. Unlicensed so B.Y.O. and corkage is free. They also do catering. No credit cards.

Much more than just a bakery

Neal's Yard Bakery

Café and organic wholemeal bakery with seating upstairs overlooking the courtyard. Soups, salads, hot dishes and desserts to eat in or take away, plus all kinds of bread. The menu changes regularly and there is always a vegan option.

Some typical soups have been roasted red pepper and garlic, or split pea and mint for £2.00 a small portion or £2.35 a regular add 35p on for eat-in. There are four salads daily and they are all vegan again with small or regular portions you can pay from £3.00 up to £3.35 depending on whether you eat-in or go.

For mains you could try the sweet potato and spinach and korma or mushroom and cashew biriyani, both vegan for £3.00 small or £3.60 regular which rises to £3.50 or £3.95 if you eat in.

They have several dessert items of which some are vegan like the fruit and nut bars or coconut cookies, plus cake of the day always sugar free and vegan for £1.10.

They don't currently have a license but this is in the pipeline. Until then B.Y.O. with free corkage. Credit cards not accepted.

Bread can be available from 6.30am in the morning when baked, although they don't actually open till about 10am.

Vegan & veggie restaurant

*6 Neal's Yard
Covent Garden
London WC2H 9DP*

Tel: 020-7836 5199

Tube: Covent Garden

*Mon-Sat:
10.30-17.00,*

Sun closed

COVENT GARDEN Vegetarian restaurants

Neal's Yard Salad Bar

Vegetarian café
and restaurant

*1–2 Neal's Yard
Covent Garden
London WC2H 9DP*

*Tel:
020–7836 3233*

*Tube:
Covent Garden,
Tottenham Ct. Rd.*

*Every day
08.30–21.00*

*www.
nealsyardsaladbar.
co.uk
(recipes)*

Vegan owned vegetarian wholefood café downstairs with tables inside and out, waiter service, and a new restaurant upstairs, with candles on the stairs to get a romantic evening off to a good start. Food is prepared in the open kitchen before your very eyes, with a Brazilian, English, Italian, Lebanese and Oriental twist.

Lots of appetisers, £1.70 eat in or £1 take–away, like vegan mini quiche with red pepper, leek and tofu; coriander rice bread. Vegan pizzas (made with soya mayonnaise) and sandwiches £1.50–£1.90 take–away or £3.20–£4.00 eat in.

Hot meals include pumpkin, leek, and polenta pie; Lebanese kibe – oven baked cracked wheat with carrot, fresh coriander, peppers and onion; stir fry rice noodles. Small £5.50 (take–away £3.50), large £6.50 (£4.00).

Lots of vegan desserts £2.00–£3.40 such as chocolate mousse, banana cinnamon cake, almond berries ginger tart.

Drinks £2–£3 include mango juice, mixed berry, Brazilian fruit shake. Portuguese and alcohol free beer.

House wine £3 a glass, £14 a bottle.

World Food Café

Upstairs international wholefood vegetarian restaurant, overlooking Neal's Yard. 90% vegan. There's an open plan kitchen in the centre so you can see all the food being prepared.

Meals from every continent £5.95 such as Indian spicy veg masala with steamed brown rice; falafel. Small mixed salad £4. Soup of the day £3.85.
Big meals £7.95 could be thali; Turkish meze; West African sweet potatoes and cabbage in creamy groundnut and cayenne sauce served with fresh banana, steamed brown rice and salad; Mexican platter; large mixed plate of all the day's salads.

Desserts £3.25–£3.45. Fresh fruit juice £1.85, herb teas (pot) £1.40, fresh lime soda £1.65, cafetiere £1.40. Minimum charge £5.00 at lunchtime and Saturdays. Close second in *Time Out* 1998 best vegetarian meal.

First Floor
14 Neal's Yard
Covent Garden
London WC2H 9DP

Tel: 020-7379-0298

Tube:
Covent Garden,
Tottenham Ct. Rd.

Mon–Fri :
11.30–16.30,

Sat: 11.30–17.00,

Sun closed

Gaby's

Mediterranean
Omnivorous

Uncomplicated omnivorous Mediterranean café close to Leicester Square tube station on the Covent Garden side of Charing Cross Rd. Stacks of veggie and vegan eat-ins and take-aways for a fiver or less. Real favourite because of its location and prices, though food can be a little on the oily side.

Point to what you want in the deli style counter, such as stuffed aubergine or pepper £5.50, pasta with herb and tomato sauce £4, excellent falafels £2.50. 20 salads £2–3. Chips £1.30.

All kinds of alcohol, coffee, lemon and herb tea.

30 Charing Cross Rd.
by Leicester Square
London WC2H 0DB

Tel: 020–7836 4233

Tube: Leicester Sq.

Mon–Sat:
11.00–24.00,
Sun: 11.00–21.00

Wagamama

Japanese
omnivorous

Omnivorous fast food Japanese noodle bar with over nine veggie and vegan dishes.

See Bloomsbury, WC1 branch for menu.

1 Tavistock Street
Covent Garden
London WC2E 7PE

Tel: 020–7836 3330

Tube: Covent Garden

Mon–Sat:
11.00–23.00

The Cafe, Students' Union LSE

Omnivorous café

Student basement café in the London School of Economics, no longer completely veggie but with several options for veggies, some vegan. These may change daily and prices are very reasonable.

*East Buildings
Basement
Houghton Street
Aldwych
London WC2 2AE*

Several veggie sandwiches and filled bagels £1 –£1.85 include veg fake chicken, houmous and salad.

Tel: 020–7955–7164

Tube: Temple

The soup of the day is always vegetarian or vegan, such as tomato and basil with mixed veg, or minestrone.

*Mon–Fri:
9.00–18.00 term,*

10.00–15.00 during holidays

Salads £1.10– £2.30 might include pasta with tomato, or couscous salad with mixed veg. The panini is also veggie – five bean with roasted veg and hummous.

Please note that opening hours vary according to term times.

Carrie Awaze Designer Sandwiches

Omnivorous
sandwich shop

27 Endell Street
Covent Garden
London WC2H 9BA

Tel: 020–7836 0815

Tube: Covent Garden

Mon–Fri:
10.00–20.00,

Sat: 12.00–19.00,

Sun 12–17.00

Omnivorous Indian and international take-away with stacks for veggies and vegans.

Soup £2.95 or take out £1.95.

6 vegan and 21 veggie sandwiches £1.95–2.95 take-away or £2.3–3.80 eat in, such as "Brown Bomber" onion bhajia with hummous and salad.

Filled jacket spud £5.95–6.25 such as "Arne Street" with dhal and onion bhajia, or with veg curry and cashews. Vegetarian thali or curry and rice £7.95.

Fresh fruit salad is the only vegan dessert.

Beer £2.25 with food. Wine £9.50 bottle or £2.25 glass. Herb tea or coffee £1.25, they have soya milk.

If you would like to find out more about the work we do and how you can become involved in helping to fight animal cruelty, please contact us at the address below.

Animal Aid
against all animal cruelty

Education   **Campaigns**
Information   **Advice**
Resources   **Investigations**
Exhibitions

Vegetarianism
Factory farming
Animal experiments
Fur trade
Pet trade
Zoos and Circuses
Living without cruelty
Humane research

**Animal Aid
The Old Chapel
Bradford Street
Tonbridge
Kent TN9 1AW
Tel:** (01732) 364546
Fax: (01732) 366533
Web: www.animalaid.org.uk

ANIMAL AID
Strictly peaceful
campaigning.

Holland & Barrett

Healthfoods &
wholefoods store

Big health food shop in Covent Garden, formerly called Neal's Yard, by the entrance to the actual Neal's Yard with its three veggie cafes. Open 7 days. They have some take-away food but for fresh organic fruit and veg you'll have to go to the nearby Tesco Metro.
They offer food allergy testing in this store, although it is advisable to phone to book.

21 Shorts Gardens
Covent Garden
London WC2H

Tel: 020-7379-0298

Tube:
Covent Garden,
Tottenham Court Rd

Mon–Sun:
10.00–19.00

Holland & Barrett

Healthfoods store

Down the left side of Charing Cross station. Lots of veggie snacks and take-aways including pies, pastries and cakes.

Unit 16,
Embankment
Shopping Centre,
Villiers St,
London WC2 6NN

Tel: 020-7839 4988

Tube: Embankment,
Charing Cross

Mon–Fri:
9.00–18.00,

Sat 9–18.00,

Sun closed

IF KILLING FOR MEAT MAKES YOU SICK...

...DON'T LET HIM BE HUNTED AND KILLED JUST FOR FUN!

If you want to help STOP this pointless killing,
support the League Against Cruel Sports now.

To join, donate, or for information on
leaving a legacy contact us today
quoting the reference: vgl

Tel: **020 7403 6155** ■ Web: **www.league.uk.com**
■ E-mail: **donate@league.uk.com**
83/87 Union Street, London SE1 1SG

LEAGUE
AGAINST CRUEL SPORTS

CAMPAIGNING
FOR WILDLIFE

BLOOMSBURY

The heart of Bloomsbury, to the right of Tottenham Court Road, is the huge **British Museum**, well worth a day at least once a year.

Our favourite road is **Marchmont Street** with lots of cafes, take-aways, a cinema nearby and a real community feel. The new Indian restaurant **Vegetarian Paradise** has replaced the mediocre previous tenant, and **Alara** wholefoods is opposite.

In Torrington Place, down the side of Barclays Bank on Tottenham Court Road, you'll find **Planet Organic** wholefood supermarket with a cafe, open on Sundays.

We've cheated a bit and included the **Drummond Street** Indian restaurants in this section, the perfect place to end your day, especially if you're about to grab a train north at Euston station. Just the other side of Tottenham Court Road is the brand new Chinese vegan buffet restaurant **Joi** in Percy Street, see Marylebone section.

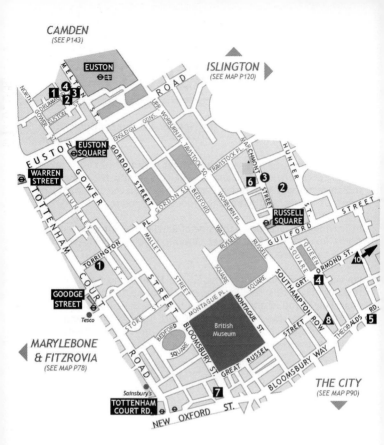

CAMDEN
(SEE P143)

ISLINGTON
(SEE MAP P120)

EUSTON

EUSTON SQUARE

WARREN STREET

GOODGE STREET

Tesco

MARYLEBONE
& FITZROVIA
(SEE MAP P78)

RUSSELL SQUARE

British Museum

THE CITY
(SEE MAP P90)

Sainsbury's

TOTTENHAM COURT RD.

NEW OXFORD ST.

NORTH GOWER

DRUMMOND

MELTON

EUSTON

ENSLEIGH GDNS

GORDON STREET

UPR WOBURN PL

WOBURN PL

TAVISTOCK SQ.

BEDFORD WAY

GORDON SQ.

TRAVISTOCK PL.

KARCHMONT STREET

HUNTER ST.

GUILFORD STREET

RUSSELL SQUARE

SOUTHAMPTON ROW

QUEEN SQUARE

GRT ORMOND ST.

THEOBALD'S RD.

STREET

EUSTON

GOWER

HUNTLEY

TORRINGTON

STREET

MALLET

STORE

BEDFORD SQUARE

MONTAGUE PL.

MONTAGUE ST.

BLOOMSBURY ST.

GREAT RUSSEL STREET

BLOOMSBURY WAY

TOTTENHAM COURT

ROAD

ISLINGTON
Stoke Newington
CAMDEN
HACKNEY
Islington
Bloomsbury
Marylebone & Fitzrovia
Covent Grdn.
City
CITY OF LONDON
TOWER HAMLET
Soho
WESTMINSTER
KENSINGTON
SOUTHWARK
LAMBETH
LEWISHAM

Bloomsbury

Places in Bloomsbury

■ Vegetarian restaurants

■ Omnivorous restaurants

▲ Coffee and bars

● Wholefood & health food shops

▲ Veggie meeting places

Chutneys

Vegetarian South Indian restaurant. With wide variety of dishes and special Keralan feast menu available most days. It's a popular place for a quiet romantic dinner that won't stretch the wallet too much.

Eat as much as you like buffet from 12 noon to 2.45pm every day for £5.45

There are 16 starters such as bhel poori, vegetable kebab, ragara pattice, £2.20 to £3.00.

Main courses include nine kinds of dosa £2.80–£E4.85, 11 curries £2.50–3.40. Plenty of whole wheat breads, pickles; salad and rice from 90p.

Thalis start at £3.95. If you are really hungry try the excellent Chutney's deluxe thali for £7.95 with dhal soup, 4 curries, pillau rice, chutneys, chappatis or pooris and dessert.

Five desserts £1.60–£1.80 but we couldn't see anything for vegans.

**Vegetarian
South Indian**

*124 Drummond Street
Euston
London NW1 2HL*

Tel: 020-7388-0604

*Tube: Euston,
Euston Square*

*Open every day
Lunch buffet
12.00–14.25,
diner through til
22.30*

Coffee Matters

Organic coffee bar

Organic coffee bar serving Fairtrade coffee, tea, hot chocolate, organic sandwiches, snacks, and cakes.

Vegan sandwiches currently available are alfalfa sprout with tomato, and houmous on tomato bread. Also falafel and salad.

4 Southampton Row
nr Holborn Tube
Holborn
London WC1

Tube: Holborn

Mon–Fri:
7.00–18.00,
Sat: 9.00–15.00,
Sun closed

Ravi Shankar

**Vegetarian
South Indian**

One of three great value vegetarian South Indian restaurants in this street next to Euston station. Similar menu to the branch in the Islington but with daily specials throughout the week. There's always plenty for vegans.

Set three course meal £6.95, two courses £5.70, or have a dosa or curry for £2 to £4.

On a Monday they serve cashew nut pillau rice and cauliflower curry for £3.95, Tuesday is veg biriyani with curry for £4.25, and each day the specials are different.

They have wine and lager. Most cards accepted.

*133–135 Drummond
Street*
Euston
London NW1 2HL

Tel: 020–7388 6458

*Tube: Euston,
Euston Square*

Open every day
12.00–22.45
(last orders 22.30)

68

Diwana Bhelpoori House

One of the larger vegetarian Indian restaurants on Drummond Street. Light wood décor and lots of potted palms give a relaxed and informal feel. The food is inexpensive and tasty. They offer an eat as much as you like lunch buffet for £4.80 which has different dishes daily, and also a full a la carte menu all day.

Lots of starters such as dahi vada chick peas £2.30, masala spring rolls £2.50.

Thalis £4.00 to £6.00.

Lots of dosas and vegetable side dishes like bombay aloo and aloo gobi starting at £2.40.

Several desserts, alas as in most Indian restaurants there is not much for vegans.

Diwana are not licensed but you can bring your own with no corkage charge. There is an off licence nearby.

They have been established for over twenty five years and can also do outside catering.

121–123 Drummond Street
Euston
London NW1 2HL

Tel: 020-7387 5556

Tube: Euston,
Euston Square,
Warren St

Open every day
12.00–23.30

BLOOMSBURY Vegetarian restaurants

Mary Ward

Vegetarian Café

Completely vegetarian cafe in an adult education centre by green Queens Square. Modern and bright with monthly changing art exhibits. Friendly Italian/Portuguese owners so expect a Mediterranean flavour on the menu which changes daily.

Breakfast served until 11.30, usually toast, jam and Danish pastries.

The lunch menu includes four salads which are all vegan and you help yourself to the dressings, £1.30 small or £2.50 large. They bake bread on the premises such as herby garlic bread.

Light meals £1.70–3.20 include stuffed baguettes, such as red lentil and olive pate with lettuce; soup (always vegan), tortilla and salsa; stir-fry noodles with veg.

Main dishes include roast veg with couscous, or roast onion stuffed with couscous and veg, with a choice of salads for £3.50.
Cakes from 80p but alas none vegan.

Plenty of cold drinks like Purdeys and Aqua Libra as well as coffees and herbal teas, soyacinno and barleycup. Not licensed.

No smoking thoughout. Cheques but no credit cards. Near London Vegans' last Wednesday venue (see Local Groups) so a great place to unwind beforehand.

42 Queen Square
Bloomsbury
London WC1N 3AQ

Tel:
020–7831 7711

Tube: Russell Sq.,
Holborn

Mon–Thur:
9.30–20.50,
Fri: 9.30–20.30,
Sat: 9.30–16.00,
Sun: closed

Vegetarian Paradise

Indian vegetarian restaurant offering real value for money with a lunch time buffet, all you can eat for £4.50 per adult.

Hot starters from £1.95 include ragara pattice, stuffed potato cakes with spicy chick peas. Cold starters like pani poori – hollow wholewheat pooris served with tamarind and dates, spicy sauces and boiled chick peas for £2.25.

Mains from £2.40 for curries or £2.50 for a plain dosa.

Woolley's Health Foods

Take-away and some wholefoods. 10 salads with raw and cooked vegan options such as organic wild rice with peanuts, parsley and red peppers in sweet pickle dressing. Vegan pies and pasties, baked potatoes, soups occasionally vegan and some cakes. Fresh every day and able to cater for gluten free. Fax your order through on 020-7430-2417.

Indian restaurant & take-away

59 Marchmont Street Bloomsbury London WC1N 1AP

Tel: 020-7278 6881

Tube: Russell Square

Mon–Sun: 12–15.00 and then 17.00–23.00

VeggieTake-Away & wholefoods shop

33 Theobalds Road London WC1X 8XP

Tel: 020-7405 3028

Tube: Holborn, Chancery Lane

Mon–Fri : 07.30–15.30, closed on Sat & Sun

Wagamama

Omnivorous
Japanese

One of ten Japanese noodle bars listed in this book, with over nine veggie and vegan dishes, long trestle tables and very noisy. Not great for a first date, but superb if you're out on the town for a laff. All dishes served together.

Raw mixed juices £2.55. Mains include veg soup with wholemeal ramen noodles, stir-fried veg and tofu £6.25; yasai katsu curry with rice, mixed leaves and pickles £6. Also two sauce based noodle dishes. Side dishes, £1.25–£4.25 like five grilled veg dumpling; miso soup; skewers of chargrilled veg coated in yakitori sauce. Extras include noodles, rice and pickles. At www.wagamama.com you can send e-cards to set up your evening.

4A Streatham Street
off Bloomsbury St.
Bloomsbury
London WC1A 1JB

Tel:
020-7323 9223

Tube:
Tottenham Court Rd.

Mon-Sat:
12-23.00,
Sun:
12-22.00

Planet Organic

Organic super-market and cafe

22 Torrington Place London WC1A 7JE

Tel: 020-7436-1929

Tube: Goodge St

Mon-Fri: 9.00-20.00, Sat: 11-18.00, Sun: 12-18.00

Organic wholefood supermarket off Tottenham Court Road, with a juice bar and café. Most dishes, snacks and cakes have ingredients displayed and if they're gluten, sugar free or vegan. All waste is recycled and even the take-away cartons are made from recycled paper.

The deli/cafe section has hot and cold dishes and salads, some of which are always vegan, for take-away or eat in at the handful of tables by the tills and outside

The shop sells everything for veggies including fifteen types of tofu and tempeh, every kind of pasta you can imagine and some you can't (spelt, quinoa) as well as lots of macrobiotic products for home sushi.

Huge section devoted to health and body care, including the Green People range which carries the Vegan Society logo, and all the products listed in our toiletries and cosmetics chapter near the end of this guide.

A great place for presents like pretty candles, incense and aromatherapy oils. They even sell *Vegetarian London, Britain, France* and *Europe*.

Staff are well-trained to deal with customer queries and have in depth knowledge of what's what.

Alara Wholefoods

Healthfoods & wholefoods store

Vegetarian healthfood shop that is very popular with the locals. Large take–away section and one of the best places to grab lunch to go. Loads of vegan and organic produce including: fruit & veg, cosmetics, food supplements, wide variety of bread, and a small selection of veggie beers and organic juices.

58 Marchmont Street
Bloomsbury
London WC1N 1AB

Tel:
020–7837 1172

Tube: Russell Square

Mon–Fri:
9.00–18.00,
Sat: 10–18.00,
Sun: closed

Holland & Barrett

Healthfoods & wholefoods store

Part of healthfood shop chain in UK, small branch with many veggie/vegan munchies like dried fruit, nuts and seeds, but no fresh take–away.

36 Brunswick
Shopping Ctr
Bloomsbury
London WC1N 1AE

Tel:
020–7278 4640

Tube:
Russell Square

Mon–Sat:
9.30–17.30,
Sun closed

Central London

Marylebone & Fitzrovia

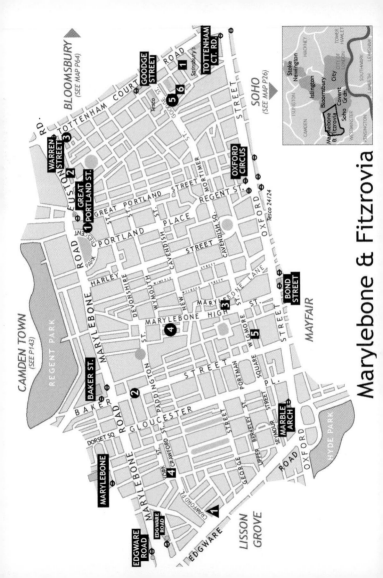

Marylebone & Fitzrovia

Places in Marylebone & Fitzrovia

■ Vegetarian restaurants

■ Omnivorous restaurants

● Wholefood & health food shops

▲ Veggie meeting places

Joi

Brand new Chinese vegan eat-as-much-as-you-like buffet, between Charlotte Street and Tottenham Court Road, specialising in fake meats and run by a relative of the proprietor of Tai in Greek Street.

£5 daytime, £6 evening, or £3 for a take-away box.

Choose from chow mein, rice, sweet and sour veg "pork" balls, soya chicken, fake beef, crispy seaweed, fried aubergine, spring rolls, tofu and many more.

A more upmarket a la carte restaurant section at the back is also planned.

Vegan Oriental restaurant

14 Percy Street
off Charlotte Street
London W1

Tel:
020-7323 -0981

Tube: Goodge Street,
Tottenham Court Rd

Open every day for
lunch and dinner

CTJ

Oriental vegan restaurant

New bargain vegan Oriental hot buffet restaurant close to Euston Station and Warren Street tubes. Eat as much as you like buffet for £5, take-out box £3. They change the menu daily and most of the dishes are vegan.

Choose from veg Thai curry, sweet and sour veg balls, lemon grass pot, spring rolls, crispy aubergine and black bean with mixed veg, seaweed spiced aubergine. There are usually several vegetable curries with tofu and all kinds of fake meats which we've seen fool carnivores. "Hey honey," said one American tourist to his vegetarian wife, "you don't wanna eat this beef."

Special offer for students – free soft drink after 3.00pm if you present a copy of this book. They are unlicensed but you can bring your own and pay a minimal charge for corkage.

339 Euston Road
London NW1 3AD

Tel: 020-7387-5450

Tube:
Great Portland St,
Warren Street,
Euston

Open every day
12.00-22.00

Woodlands

Perhaps the largest vegetarian Indian chain in the world, with 3 London branches.

Starters like idli rice balls, or deep fried cashew nut pokoda, £2.95 to £3.75.

Nine varieties of dosa (vegetable stuffed pancake) from £3.95 to £5.50. Their specialty is uthappam or lentil pizza, with coconut, tomato, green chilli for £4.50, extra toppings 25p. 10 curries from £3.95 to £4.95

Thalis or set meals £12.50–£13.50.

Many rice dishes such as lemon or coconut, £1.95 to £4.95. Indian breads like bathura £1.95.

7 desserts with some unusual ones like Jaggary dosa; an Indian crepe filled with pure sugar cane and cardamom at £3.75; Sheera – cream of wheat with nuts, raisins and ghee for £3.50.

Glass of house wine £3.25, bottle £9.50 . Beer £2.50.

They accept most major credit cards and cater for parties.

Vegetarian
Indian restaurant.

*77 Marylebone Lane
(off Marylebone High
St.)
London W1M 4GA*

*Tel:
020–7486 3862*

*Tube:
Bond St./Baker St.*

*7 days a week for
lunch from 12.30
and dinner 18.00–
23.00.*

Raw Deal

All day week day vegetarian cafe handy for Baker Street and Madame Tussauds.

Seasonal menu changes daily with a soup and at least two hot dishes, lots of salads and great vegan cakes, in fact there are always plenty of choices for vegans.

Veggie breakfast with mushrooms on toast, beans, tomatoes, fresh juice and tea or coffee for £3.50.

Asparagus soup £2.20. 10 salads £1.25 per portion or four for £4.00. Jacket potatoes with fillings.

Main courses £6.00–£6.50 come with 2 salads, for example rissoles with hot vegetables; ratatouille with butterbeans; Chinese style veg and stir-fried noodles. There is usually a pasta dish of the day.

Many of the cakes are vegan £2.00–£2.50.

Coffees and herbal teas, with soya milk always available. Glass of house wine£1.95, bottle £12.50. Beer £2.95.

Cheques, luncheon vouchers, but no credit cards.

Party catering if you collect.

vegetarian café/restaurant

65 York Street, off Seymour Place Marylebone London W1H 1PQ

Tel: 020–7262–4841

Tube: Baker Street

Mon–Fri: 08.00–22.00

Closed Sat–Sun.

MARYLEBONE TO FITZROVIA Vegetarian restaurants

Omnivorous restaurants

Rasa Express

Unlike their restaurant in parallel Charlotte Street, here most of the menu is veggie snacks and take-aways.

Typical snacks for £1.50 are Mysore potato balls with ginger curry leaves, coriander and black mustard seeds, fried in chickpea flour; or crispy spongy dumpling in a crunchy case made from urad beans and chillies, with coconut chutney.

Take-aways £2-£2.50 like masala dosa (vegetable stuffed pancake) or vegetable biriyani.

Veggie & fish
Indian

5 Rathbone Street
Off Oxford Street
London W1

Tel: 020-7637-0222

Tube: Tottenham Ct.Rd.

12-3pm buffet

Wagamama

Large omnivorous Japanese fast food noodle restaurant, this was the third to open in London, they now have ten.

See Bloomsbury, WC1 branch for menu.

Omnivorous
Japanese

101A Wigmore St
London W1H 9AB

Tel: 020 7409 0111

Tube:
Marble Arch, Bond St

Mon-Sat:12.00-23.00,
Sun: 12.00-22.00

Holland & Barrett

Part of the national chain, this is a medium sized shop with a wide range of supplements, plus some take-away foods.

Health food shop

78 Baker St
London W1M 1DL

Tel: 020-7935 3544

Tube: Baker St.

Mon-Fri: 8.30-18.00,
Sat: 9.00-17.30,
Sun closed

Nutri Centre Ltd.

In the basement of a natural health centre, this shop sells mainly supplements and body care products, plus a few foods like pasta

There is a big books section with a separate telephone: 020-7323 2382. They have an impressive mail order books catalogue.

Cruelty free
cosmetics & food

7 Park Crescent
London W1N

Tel: 020-7436-5122

Tube:
Regents Park,
Great Portland St

Mon-Fri: 9.00-18.30,
Sat 10-16.00,
Sun closed

Health Food Centre

11 Warren Street
Euston
London NW1

Tel: 020-7387 9289

Tube: Warren Street

Mon-Fri:
8.30-19.00,
Sat 12.00-16.00

Vegetarian health food shop and take-away tucked away down the side of Warren Street tube. The owner Raj is very friendly and a committed veggie and has recently added a juice and coffee bar with a table outside, weather permitting. Handy for Euston or Regents Park.

London's biggest range of veggie and vegan sandwiches, like (fake) chicken and salad, lentil burger and houmous with salad, date, walnut and banana, veggie burger and houmous, or veggie BLT. Plus filled topedos, baps and baguettes.All £2.60 for two which is stunning value for central London.

Savouries like spicy Mexican slice, cartons of pasta and couscous salad. Hot take-away dishes include brown rice and curry, and pasta bake.

Lots of cakes, some sugar free or suitable for vegans like date crumble.

The juice bar has combos like apple, ginger and orange feor £1.30 medium, £1.99 large. Energy drinks like spirulina, echinacea or guarana around £2.50. Wheat-grass £1.60 a shot. Vegan fruit smoothie £1.40. Coffee, teas and soyacinno £1.00 for a largish cup.

Extensive range of cruelty-free toiletries and herbal remedies and oils.

GNC

Mainly vitamins and supplements at this shop, not much food apart from soya milk and rice cakes.

Health food shop

104 Marylebone High Street,
London W1

Tel:
020-7935 -3924

Tube:
Baker Street

Mon-Fri:
9.00-19.00,

Sat: 9.00- 18.00,

Sun: 12.00-17.00

Peppercorn's

Brand new organic whole food store selling everything for veggies including tofu and tempeh, every kind of pasta and health food. Take-away and macrobiotic specialities from around the world, some organic, with lots of vegan options including Mexican bean slices, vegetarian rotis, country pies, vegetarian sushi, spinach filo pastries, tofu parcels, rice rolls, organic hummous, cottage pies, veggie sausages, rice and curry, cakes and flapjacks. Most dishes, snacks and cakes have ingredients displayed and if they're gluten, sugar free or vegan. Also supplements, vitamins and minerals, plus Ecover cleaning products. Staff are well trained and have in depth knowledge of what's what.

Wholefood shop

2 Charlotte Place,
London W1

Tel:
020-7631 4528

Tube:
Goodge Street

Mon-Fri:
09.00-19.00,

Sat: 11.00- 18.00,

Sun: closed

10% discount for Vegetarian or Vegan Society

Central London
The City

ISLINGTON
(SEE MAP P120)

City of London

Places in the City

Carnevale

Vegetarian restaurant, snack bar and take-away with a glass roofed area out back.

The take-away menu has over 20 items with salads, sandwiches like houmous, mushroom paté, or aubergine and peppers with sun-dried tomatoes £2.50.

A la carte menu includes vegan soup of the day £3.50, aubergine dip with spinach and spicy chick peas £4.75. Main courses £9 such as marinated bean curd and vegetables in Thai sweet chilli sauce with buckwheat noodles, or baked poblano chilli stuffed with sweet potato and wild mushroom served with sweet potato.

Five desserts £4.25.

Wine £9.95 bottle, £2.70.glass, organic £11.25/£2.95. Hot and cold drinks from 90p. No credit cards. Local deliveries if you order the day before.
Menu at www.carnevalerestaurant.co.uk

Mediterranean restaurant

135 Whitecross St.
London EC1Y 8JL

Tube: Old Streeet,
Barbican

Tel:
020–7250 3452

Monday–Friday:
10 am–10 pm

Saturday:
17.30 pm–22.30 pm

Futures!!

Big vegetarian cafe with international cuisine that becomes a bar in the evenings. On the edge of Liverpool Street station in Exchange Square, free from traffic. Plenty for vegans except dessert.

Extensive eat-in and take-away breakfast menus from 07.30-10.30am including muesli £1.80 eat in (£1.20 take-away), full cooked English breakfaset £5.25, or portions at 95p each. 9 vareieties of £1.30 (70p) and 7 kinds of coffee. Lots of pastries too.

The lunch menu changes monthly with daily specials. Soup of the day with roll £2.95. Four salads at £2.20 each or combos for £5.50, such as puy lentil and spicy coriander with lime dressing, or mixed leaves with olive oil vinaigrette.

Hot dishes include stir-fry veg with noodles, or vegetable hot pot in cider with rice, £6.50. Pasta dishes and bakes like shepherdess pie from £2.10.

Several desserts, though only fruit salad was vegan, £1.80 to £2.95.

Fruit smoothies like mangomania and blueberry breeze for £2.75.

Smoke free before 2pm. They stop serving food at 3pm and become a bar, but in the evening they have some snacks. They accept credit cards and there is a service charge of 12% for parties of 5 and over after work.

Big vegetarian café & evening bar

2 Exchange Square
Off Primrose Street
London EC2A 2EH

Tel:
020-7638 6341

Tube:
Liverpool Street

Mon-Fri:
07.30-22.00
(Fri 23.00),

bar only from 3pm.

Closed at weekends

THE CITY   Vegetarian restaurants

Futures!! – supping in the City

Futures!

This Futures is vegetarian take-away only, in a secluded pedestrianised alley in the heart the City. Similar menu to the bigger branch and heaps of things for vegans.

Soup of the day might be cream of pea with mint £2.10.

Choose from several hot dishes £4 like the bake of the day, fusilli with spinach and mushroom in a tomato and basil sauce, or stir fry veg with rice.

Four salads like mixed bean, or cabbage, apple and raisin with grain mustard dressing, or mixed leaves, cucumber, mustard and cress with dill dressing, all vegan. £1.30 single portion, £3 combos.

Desserts £1.80 include apricot bakewell tart.

Smoothies sold here as well as tea, coffee and juices.

Daily changing menu faxed out nightly to 200 companies and city tycoons can check it on Reuters City Screen LOLO L852/853 then order by phone. See EC2 for breakfast menu. Credit cards accepted on orders over £15 delivered.

Parties and outside functions catered.

Vegetarian take-away

8 Botolph Alley
Eastcheap
London EC3R 8DR

Tel:
020-7623 4529

Tube: Monument

Mon-Fri: breakfast
07.30-10.00,

lunch: 11.30-15.00.

THE CITY Vegetarian restaurants

The Place Below in the crypt of St Mary-le-Bow Church

The Place Below

Veggie restaurant
& take-away

Crypt of St Mary-le-Bow Church
The City, London
EC2V 6AU

Tel:
020-7329 0789

Tube: St Paul's

Mon-Fri
07.30-15.30,

lunch
11.30-14.30

Located in the Norman Crypt of a Wren church, this large vegetarian restaurant provides a quiet retreat. 80 seats inside plus 40 in the churchyard. Global food, especially Mediterranean and Middle Eastern. Menu changes daily.

Soup £2.20 take-away, £2.90 inside.

Salads, £5.50 take-away, £7.50 eat in like tabouleh, lemon spiced carrots, aubergine puree and marinated green beans in tomato dressing.

The hot dish of the day £4.50 might be ratatouille with Asian flavours, spiced chickpeas and coconut rice. Discount on the dish of the day 11.30am-12pm.

They offer a healthbowl at £5.50 eat-in containing wholegrain rice, puy lentils, vegetables, leaves, herbs and soy balsamic dressing.

Desserts like apple, raspberry and almond cake, £2.80 in or £2.20 to go.

Special morning deal 7.30-11.30a.m.: any hot drink including soyacinnos, hot chocolate, teas and lattes for 50p a cup.

Bring your own booze, no corkage charge. No smoking. Visa, MC.

Available for private hire evenings.

Ravi Shankar's

Vegetarian South Indian restaurant close to Saddlers Wells theatre, owned by the same folk as the Ravi Shankar in Drummoned Street and with a similar but not identical menu.

Eat as much as you like lunchtime buffet for an inflation proof £4.50 noon–2.15pm, including dessert.

Starters £2.30–£2.75 include vegetable kebab, potato bonda, aloo chana chat and dahi vada.

Main dishes £3.10–£4.60 include uthappam with coconut chutney; masala dosa, deluxe rava dosa.

Choose from 10 Sabzi or side dishes such as Bombay aloo, mixed veg curry or saag bhajee, pickles, chutneys and salads 60p to £3.25.

The set meal or Thali goes up to £6.95 for a complete 3 course meal.

Bring your own alcohol, free corkage. There's an off-license nearby. Vegan friendly as vegetable, not butter, ghee is used. Booking advised. Visa, MC.

Vegetarian South Indian restaurant

422 St John's Street
Islington
London EC1

Tel:
020–7833 5849

Tube: Angel

Mon–Sat:
12.00–14.30,
18–23.00

Sun:
12–18.00 buffet,
18–22.45 a la carte

JJ's Wrap Kitchen

**Vegetarian
fast food**

Brand new vegetarian fast food, which helps to make up for the loss of Crazy Salads at Moorgate and Holborn. Like many new veggie places in their first year, they use a lot of dairy or egg.

Four kinds of wraps £2.99–£4.29 such as Lebanese falafel.

Soup of the day £2.49, miso £1.39.

Chunky chips from £1.69. Crispy hot gyoza Japanese dumplings with sweet chilli dip from £2.49.

Side salad £1.99.

Drinks and smoothies.

20 seats with 15 more outside in summer.

No smoking or alcohol.

Call for deliveries.

*Citypoint
1 Ropemaker Street
London EC2*

Tel: 020–7427–6007

*Tube: Moorgate,
Liverpool Street*

*Mon–Fri :
07.30–18.30,*

Sat–Sun closed

*www.
jjswrapkitchen.co.uk*

CTB

Completely vegetarian/vegan oriental buffet restaurant in the heart of the city.

All you can eat for £5.00 (all day) or you can have a take-away for £3.00 a box.

The dishes change daily but you can expect a typical range to include veg Thai curry, sweet and sour veg balls, lemon grass pot, spring rolls, crispy aubergine and black bean with mixed veg, seaweed spiced aubergine, several tasty veg curries with tofu and all kinds of fake meats.

They are licensed for alcohol.

88 Leather Lane
The City
London EC1

Tel: 020-7242-6128

Tube: Moorgate

Mon–Fri :
12.00–22.00,

Sat–Sun:
17.30–22.00

Wheatley's

Veggie family run café and flower shop with friendly vegetarian proprietors Jane and mum, not far from Saddlers Wells. There is garden with canopy for summer showers and heaters in winter. Plenty for vegans.

Soup £2.10. Sandwiches made to order. Around 15 salads, small £2.75, medium £3.50, large £5.00.

Many hot lunch possibilities £2.50–£4.00 including tortillas, savoury crepes and falafel wraps.

Vegan cakes £1.50.

Freshly squeezed juices, smoothies, herbal teas

They have a small stock of health foods, some of which are gluten-free or organic.

Seating outside for 15, inside for about 10. They welcome parties and office lunches.

33–34 Myddelton Street,
London EC1R 1UA

Tel:
020-7278-6662

Tube:
Angel, then 38 or 341 bus

Mon–Fri:
8.00–16.00

THE CITY Vegetarian restaurants

The Greenery

Vegetarian café &
take–away

5 Cowcross St
London EC1M 6DR

Tel: 020–7490 4870

Tube: Farringdon

Mon–Fri:
07.00–15.00.

Closed Sat–Sun.

Busy wholefood vegetarian café with big take–away trade near Farringdon tube, now with a juice bar. 50% vegan.

Breakfast with muesli, croissant, fruit scones, chocolate croissant, toast etc.

Soup £1.25 small, £2.30 large. Filled baps £1.80–£2.10. 10 salads £1.60–£3.25.

Mains £1.90–£2.95 like Homity pie, pasta, curries, veggie satay.

Desserts are mostly cakes plus fruit salad.

Fresh juices £1.50, £2.00, £2.75 and they have wheatgrass.

You can phone, fax or e–mail your order through before 11am.

Rye Wholefoods

Take–away &
wholefoods

35a Mydletton Street
London EC1R

Tel: 020–7278 5878

Wholefood store with a take–away section with vegetarian hot dishes, many of them vegan. Plus sandwiches, salads, bagels, hot and cold drinks. Small seating area inside the shop.

Fresh and Wild

Large wholefood store selling a huge range of organic fruit & veg, herbs, veggie/vegan wine and beer, cosmetics, toiletries, books, vitamins and herbal remedies.

Lots of take-away snacks and sandwiches, pies, wraps, cakes, hot soup, and salad bar. Many items vegan.

Big noticeboard advertising local events.

Regular sampling sessions like skin-care ranges and new product tasting.

Above the store is the Open Centre, which has alternative therapies, workshops and talks. Flyers for practitioners and events are in the store.

Wholefoods store

194 Old Street
The City London
EC1V 9FR

Tel:
020-7250 1708

Tube: Old St.

Mon-Fri:
9.30-19.30,

Sat:11.30-17.30,

Sun closed

Antimony Balance

Healthfoods &
wholefoods store

With large vitamin range. Also have veggie sarnies, pies and pastries nuts and seeds and delicious flapjacks. Formerly 'London Distributors'.

*47 Farringdon Road
London EC1M*

*Tel:
020-7404-5237*

Tube: Farringdon

*Mon–Fri:
8.30–18.15,
Sat & Sun closed*

Holland & Barrett

Healthfoods &
wholefoods store

Part of national chain, this small store packs a lot in. Nibbles such as dried friut and nuts, also vegan chocolate, flapjacks, supplements also some toiletries, tooth-paste and chiller cabinet with vegan yogurts.

*139-140 Cheapside
London EC2V 6BJ*

*Tel:
020-6700-7415*

*Mon–Fri:
8.00–18.00,
Sat–Sun closed*

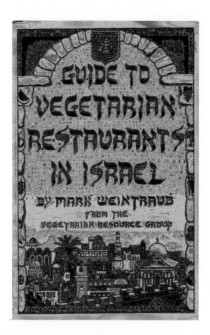

VEGETARIAN ISRAEL by Mark Weintraub

Jerusalem, Tel Aviv, Jaffa, Haifa, Tiberias, Galilee resorts, Moshav Amirim, and top winter destination Eilat on the Red Sea. Indispensable for the vegetarian, health-concerned, or kosher traveller. Restaurants range from Italian to Indian; from cafe and nightlife to upscale hotel and resort. Includes health food stores in Jerusalem, Tel Aviv and Haifa.

£6.99 + postage, mail order only from Vegetarian Guides
See order form at the end of this guide or
www.vegetarianguides.com

The Sloane Zone

Lying between Hyde Park and the River Thames are the wealthy areas of Belgravia, Knightsbridge and Chelsea, home to embassies, **Harrods**, the **Science Museum**, **Victoria & Albert Museum**, fashion stores along the King's Road, and the infamous IT girls – the blonde offspring of the self-made rich.

The classy vegan Chinese restaurant that kept changing its name (Red, Veg, Veg Veg, Ch'i), tucked away at 8 Egerton Garden Mews near Harrods, has recently become a regular omnivorous Thai (with veggie options). Apart from **Brothers Green Cafe**, when it comes to purely vegetarian restaurants this area is almost as empty as an IT girl's head.

There are however stacks of health food stores and the surrounding areas offer options, for example the Lebanese restaurants around Kensington High Street, W8, or the new Indian vegetarian restaurant Sagar in Hammersmith, W6. Or just head for the West End after your sightseeing.

Places in the Sloane Zone

Vegetarian restaurants

Omnivorous restaurants

Wholefood shops

The Brothers Green Café

New vegetarian café in the Arts Centre at the south-west end of King's Road, with many organic dishes and plenty for vegans. Brothers Marc and Simon bring culinary expertise from their global travels. Seating inside and on the terrace.

They serve an unbeatable vegan breakfast (all day) of scrambled tofu, baked beans, veggie sausage and toast with tea or coffee for £2.95. Mexican breakfast is tortilla, beans, scrambled tofu and salsa £3.50.

Soup of the day, generally vegan, with warm ciabatta, baguette or organic wholemeal bread for £2.95. Lots of bagels, wraps and sandwiches around £2.50, such as veggie sausage, mustard and roasted onion; VLT veggie sausage, lettuce, tomato and mayo; houmous with black olives, red onions and alfalfa.

Pasta of the day, various jacket potatoes with fillings like veggie sausage and beans served with salad at £3.75-£4.95. Also Mexican burrito, sweet potato wedges and salad, veggie burger, Thai curry and fragrant rice, between £3.75 and £4.75.

Dutch apple tart or fruit crumble, soya ice-cream and fresh fruit salad £1 to £2.35.

Alcohol is available when the theatre is open. They sell their own dressings and cater for outside parties.

Vegetarian café

*Chelsea Arts Centre
World's End Place,
King's Road
Chelsea
London SW10 0DR*

Tel: 020-7352-3535

*Tube:
Fulham Broadway*

*Mon-Fri:
9.00-20.00,*

Sat: 9.00-14.00,

Sun closed

Brothers Green vegetarian cafe, Chelsea

Organic Café

Veggie cafe at the back of an auction room offering a very different Sunday out. English and Thai dishes prepared by the vegan Thai proprietor Vip.

Main course for under £5, combination salad £3, main course and salad £4.95. Try Thai stir-fry rice noodles (pad Thai), vegetarian shepherd's pie, hot pot, lasagne, moussaka, vegan spicy samosas and vegan sausage rolls.

Soup £2.50 with seed loaf. Teas 70p, coffee and alternatives 90p, organic cakes like lemon, chocolate, banana (vegan) £1.35.

The café is inside the auction rooms where antiques are being sold, and it cannot be seen from the street. The cafe used to be open Friday to Monday, but at the time of going to press the Auction Rooms said they were currently only opening on Sundays.

The Auction Rooms
71 Lots Road
Chelsea
London SW10

Tel: 020-7351 7771

Tube:
Fulham Broadway

Sun only during sale from 10am onwards

SLOANE ZONE Vegetarian restaurants

111

Wagamama

Omnivorous fast food Japanese noodle bar with over nine veggie and vegan dishes.

See Bloomsbury, WC1 branch for menu.

*Omnivorous
Japanese*

*Lower Ground Floor,
Harvey Nichols
109–125
Knightsbridge*

*Knightsbridge
London SW1X 7RJ*

Tel: 020–7201 8000

Tube: Knightsbridge

*Mon–Sat:
12.00–23.00,*

Sun 12–22.30

Greens Foods

Health food shop with a wide range of veggie hot and cold take-away snacks with an Eastern flavour and also a salad bar. Gluten-free range and vegan snacks, as well as toiletries and books.

Health food shop & take-away

11-13 Strutton Ground
off Victoria Street
London SW1P

Tel: 020-7222-4588

Tube: Victoria

Mon-Sat: 7.00-18.00,

Health Craze

Health food shop that has similar range to their sister shop in Old Brompton Road.

Health food shop

115 Earls Court Road
Earls Court
London SW5

Tel: 020-7244-7784

Tube: Earls Court

Mon-Sat: 10.00-23.00
Sun: 14.00-23.00

Health Craze

Health food shops with plenty of take-away food like sandwiches, pasties and samosas, also mobile munchies like dried fruit, nuts and seeds. Good selection of cruelty-free cosmetics like BWC range, Weleda and Dead Sea Magik.

Health food shop & take-away

24 Old Brompton Rd.
South Kensington
London SW7

Tel: 020-7589-5870

Mon-Sat: 8.45-19.45,
Sun closed

Health Foods

Health food shop with take-away snacks some vegan. They have a freezer section with vegan ice-cream. Cruelty free toiletries like Dead Sea Magik.

Homeopathic practitioner available by appointment on Tuesday and Thursday mornings. 10% discount to senior citizens Thurday and Friday, and for everyone Saturday 9-10a.m. Connected to the Aetherius Society.

Health food shop & take away

767 Fulham Road London SW6

Tel: 020-7736 8848.

Mon-Sat: 9.00-17.30,

Sun closed

Holland & Barrett

Health food store at the back of Victoria rail station upstairs in the shopping centre where you can stock up on dried fruit and nuts, small soya milk cartons, vegan chocolate and other supplies on the way to the National Express coach station for Britain and Europe. There is a branch of Books Etc nearby for your travel guides.

Health food shop

Unit 15, Victoria Place Shopping Ctr Buckingham Palace Rd London SW1W 9SA

Tel: 020-7828-5480

Tube: Victoria

Mon-Sat: 08.00-20.00,

Sun 11-17.00

Holland & Barrett

Health food store with lots of supplements and snacks.

Health food shop

220 Fulham Rd
London SW10 9NB

Tel: 020-7352 9939

Mon-Fri: 9.30–18.00,
Sat: 9.30–5.30,
Sun closed

Holland & Barrett

Small take-away selection and a wide range of supplements.

Health food shop

10 Warwick Way
Pimlico
London SW1V 1QT

Tel: 020-7834-4796

Pimlico

Mon Sat: 10.00–18.00,
Sun closed

Holland & Barrett

Health food store with lots of veggie snacks.

Health food shop

192 Earls Court Rd
London SW5 9QF

Tel: 020-7370 6868

Mon-Sat:10.00–19.00
Sun closed

Holland & Barrett

Health food shop

As well as the usual foods, this store also offers monthly allergy testing. Call ahead to check times and days.

73 Kings Road
Chelsea
London SW3 4NX

Tel: 020–7352 4130

Mon–Sat: 9.00–19.00,
Sun: 11.00–17.00

Montignac Boutique

Wholefood
shop and café

Wholefood shop and café, with nothing refined, no sugar, adhering to the 'Montignac method'. Freshly cooked daily hot and cold take-away with some choices for veggies and vegans. It's not all veggie, this applies to the wines too.

160 Old Brompton Rd
South Kensington
London SW5

Tel: 020–73702010

Mon–Fri:8.30–21.00,
Sat: 8.30–18.00,
Sun: 10.00–18.00

Revital Health Place

Health food shop

Health food shop between Victoria coach and train station with macrobiotic foods and a large range of sea vegetables. Also vegan desserts, pasties, pizza and cakes. Nelsons products and lots of books. A great place to stock up before a coach journey.

Nutritionist based at shop on Wednesdays.

3a The Colonnades
123-151 Buckingham
Palace Rd
London SW1W

Tel: 020-7976-6615

Tube: Victoria

Mon–Fri: 9.00–19.00,
Sat: 9.00–18.00,
Sun closed

Naturally

Massive organic supermarket, with a coffee and juice bar, boasting 3,000 product lines. Many of them are suitable for veggies and vegans although it does have a large organic meat counter. They sell various veggie snacks, such as sandwiches which can be vegan, and tofu wiener sausages (vegan and gluten free), vegan cheese, soya-milk, pulses and ready meals. Also hemp bars and veggie salads, vegan yogurts and ice-cream. They stock veggie supplements like Solgar, the Green People range of body and baby products, and organic baby foods. Free local delivery over £80.

Organic supermarket

899-901 Fulham Road
Fulham
London SW6 5HU

Tel::
020-7736-1144

Tube: Parsons Green

Mon–Sat:
9.00–19.00,

Sun: 11.00–17.00

Queens Health Shop

Health food shop with large selection of vitamins, skin-care and body -products, also organic ranges and pre-packed veggie/vegan food to take away (but no fresh food available). They also stock BWC cosmetics.

Health food shop

64 Gloucester Road
London SW7 4QT

Tel: 020-7584-4815

Mon–Fri:
9.00–18.30,

Sat: 9.00–17.30,

Sun closed

Islington

Gateway to north London, home of Tony Blair and some cracking new vegetarian eateries, Islington is a somewhat swanky shopping area that's great for designer gifts, antiques and the farmers' market in Camden Market (not the one in Camden Town further west) on Upper Street. Some shops in Chapel Market (fruit and veg) have bargain non-leather jackets, e.g. Surprise Surprise. You can fill up afterwards at **Indian Veg Bhelpuri**, the cheapest all-you-can-eat buffet in London, or the new **SASA** Chinese vegan buffet opposite Angel tube.

Near King's Cross Station is Tony's brilliant health food store and cafe. For a quick fill up when changing tubes or trains, on the map (6) is a chip shop with falafels, on your left as you exit Kings Cross station. Opposite the station is another fast food place where you can get hummous and salad in pitta bread.

HIGHBURY &
ISLINGTON

ST PAUL'S RD.

CANONBURY

STOKE
NEWINGTON
(SEE MAP P132)

❶

LIVERPOOL

STREET

ESSEX RD.

RD.

NEW NORTH RD.

CAMDEN TOWN
(SEE MAP P143)

❷

ROAD

ST. PANCRAS RD.

CALEDONIAN ROAD

ROAD

UPPER

ESSEX

Sainsbury's

❸

CHAPEL   ❹ MARKET   ❶

❸   ❺

ANGEL

KING'S CROSS

❹

PENTONVILLE   RD.

CITY RD.

ST. JOHN

❷

ST. PANCRAS

❻

Almeida theatre

BLOOMSBURY
(SEE MAP P64)

Islington

Places in Islington

■ Vegetarian restaurants

■ Omnivorous restaurants

● Wholefood & health food shops

SASA

Yet another new Chinese vegan eat-as-much-as-you-like buffet, right opposite Angel tube station.

£5 daytime, £6 evening, or £3 for a take-away box.

Choose from chow mein, rice, sweet and sour veg "pork" balls, soya chicken, fake beef, crispy seaweed, fried aubergine, spring rolls, tofu and many more.

13 Islington High St
Islington
London N1

Tel: 020-7837 7767

Tube: Angel

Open:
every day for
lunch and dinner

Vegetarian restaurants **ISLINGTON**

Patisserie Bliss

Vegetarian French patisserie and boulangerie with seating inside and take-aways.

They serve a range filled croissants, filo parcels and puff pastry, as well as sweet items such as almond croissants and cakes. Unfortunately at the time of writing they do not have one exciting vegan treat, but we hope that will change when they find page 337 so we can include them in the next edition.

Various continental coffees.

Non-smoking thoughout.

Vegetarian French patisserie

428 St. Johns Street Junction of Upper St. & Pentonville Rd Islington London EC1V 4NJ

Tel: 020-7837-3720

Tube: Angel

Mon-Fri : 8.00-18.00,

Sat 8.30-18.00,

Sun: 9.00-16.00

ISLINGTON Vegetarian restaurants

123

Indian Veg in Chapel Market, all you can eat for £3.50

Indian Vegetarian Bhelpuri House

Best value veggie restaurant in London with a great bargain all-you-can-eat-buffet that runs all day long. Fantastic value for money here on the edge of trendy Islington, where you could easily stretch your wallet beyond the total bill here by going to nearby Upper Street for just starters or a couple of drinks. Indian Veg promotes the benefits of a vegetarian diet and were serving organic brown rice long before it ever got fashionable in this part of town. Come to think of it, how many Indian restaurants can you think of that even serve it or have non-dairy lassi?

Eat as much as you like for £3.50 from the buffet which has 3 types of rice, 3 curries, onion bhaji, poori, 3 sauces and lentil dhal. You can go back as many times as you like.

If you prefer a la carte there are snacks and starters from £1.95 like veg kebab or brinjal (aubergine slices) deep fried in gram flour. Mains include five thalis £3.95, dosas £3.50.

One of the few Indian restaurants that will make fresh vegan lassi for you in three different flavours. They even some vegan desserts (other Indian restaurants please note!), and so are a popular restaurant with London Vegans.

They use vegetable oil not butter ghee. Not licensed so B.Y.O. MC and Visa only. Smoke free zone.

92-93 Chapel Market
Islington
London N1 9EX

Tel: 020-7837 4607

Tube: Angel

Every day 11.00-23.00

ISLINGTON

Vegetarian restaurants

Tony's Natural Foods

Busy and friendly vegetarian wholefood store, basement café and organic juice bar not far from Kings Cross and the new Almeida Theatre. Seating downstairs where you can relax with friends over lunch. Herb garden out back that seats 40 with a huge 150 year old fig tree.

Different soup every day £1.15 or £2.10 Take-away hot food (mostly vegan or wheat free and organic) £2.75 medium, E3.90 large, like mung bean pie, vegetable pie, coconut. Add 75p to eat in. 14 types of organic salads £8 a kilo, all freshly made each day. Big piece of organic pie, sandwiches and baps, or falafel in a bap all £2.35. Cakes, some vegan, £1.25-1.50 like apple and date or chocolate, banana and almond.

Spirulina smoothies with freshly made nut milk including almonds, Brazils, hemp, sunflower and pumpkin seeds and linseeed oil (great for Omega essential fatty acids), £2.50 (8 oz) or £4.50 (16 oz). Juice bar in the summer.

Also wholefoods, supplements and cruelty-free toiletries. They specialise in hemp food and clothing and colourful shoulder bags, plus an extensive supply of literature on the history of hemp products, its production and beneficial uses.
Talks are held on a variety of topics, usually downstairs or in the garden (in summer) – phone Tony for details.

Vegetarian
wholefoods café

*10 Caledonian Road
Kings Cross
London N1 9DU*

Tel: 020-7837 5223

Tube: Kings Cross

*Mon–Fri
8.00–18.00,*

Sat 10.00–17.00,

Sun closed

Candid Café

Climb the stairs to get to this lofty arthouse style omnivorous café just behind the Angel tube station. Faded renaissance interior with red velvet and chipped gold leaf chairs, with some very interesting pieces of art work to gaze at!

Several veggie offerings like stuffed aubergine with herbs and veg for £5.00, which comes with salad. Also broccoli soup (vegan) with bread for £3.50. The menu changes daily.

Several sweets £3.50 such as cakes, but none vegan. Coffee £1.50, tea and herbal teas £1.

3 Torrens Street
Islington
London EC1V 1NQ

Tel: 020–7278 9368

Tube: Angel

Mon–Sat:
12.00–22.00,

Sun: 12.00–17.00

ISLINGTON Vegetarian restaurants

Barnsbury Health Foods

Wholefoods, cruelty-free cosmetics, vegan supplements. Take-away with vegan pasties and various veggie snacks. Vegan ice-cream and yoghurts.

*285 Caledonian Road
London N1*

Tel: 020-7607 7344

Tube: Kings Cross

*Mon-Sat:
8.30-18.30,*

Sun closed

GNC (General Nutrition Centre)

Health food shop

Health food shop (part of chain) that specialises in supplements and some herbal remedies, not necessarily veggie though. Take-away section with sandwiches and snacks, vegan pastries including Mexican bean slice and veggie-burger. Also gluten-free products such as cakes and bread.

Dried products, nut roasts, soya milks, veggie sausages, vegan ice-creams, some cruelty-free toiletries.

*212 Upper Street
Islington
London N1 1RL*

*Tel:
020-7226 3422*

*Tube:
Highbury and
Islington*

*Mon-Fri:
9.00-19.00,*

Sat: 9.00-18.00,

closed Sun

Holland & Barrett

This shop has a small take-away section with sandwiches and pastries and also a chiller cabinet with vegan ice-cream, vegan yogurt, veggie sausages and fishless fishcakes.

This is currently the only health food shop near the Angel, although a Planet Organic is due in some time in early 2002 located close to Chapel Market.

Health food shop

31 Upper St
Islington
London N1 0PN

Tel: 020-7359 9117

Tube: Angel

Mon-Sat:
9.00-17.30,

Sun: 11.00-16.00

Stoke Newington

The vegetarian republic of Stoke Newington has to be one of the best areas to live if you're into cruelty free living. Although not on the tube, it's smack in the middle of north London and quite easy to get to by train or bus. There are some excellent parks nearby.

Stoke Newington Church Street has a huge **Fresh & Wild** store, and lots of great eateries of which the Keralan Indian vegetarian **Rasa** is our favourite.

Omnivorous options include include Yum Yum (Thai) and Shamsudeen's (see pages 313–4).

HARINGEY

MANOR ROAD

ABNEY PARK

STOKE NEWINGTON

ROAD

LORDSHIP PARK

GREEN

CLISSOLD PARK

6

STOKE NEWINGTON

ROAD

CHURCH

1
1 STREET

3

CASANOVE

STOKE NEWINGTON HIGH

5

LANES

ALBION

HACKNEY
((SEE EAST END P206))

HIGHBURY

4
3

BERESFORD RD.

NEWINGTON GREEN

CANONBURY

BALLS

2

POND ROAD

DALSTON KINGSLAND

ROAD

SOUTHGATE RD.

ESSEX

ISLINGTON
(SEE MAP P120)

2

Stoke Newington

HARINGEY   ISLINGTON   HACKNEY

CAMDEN

Stoke
Newington

Islington

Bloomsbury
Marylebone
& Fitzrovia

City

CITY OF
LONDON

TOWER
HAMLETS

Covent
Grdn.

Soho

WESTMINSTER

SOUTHWARK

KENSINGTON   LAMBETH   LEWISHAM

Places in Stoke Newington

Rasa

Top notch vegetarian Kerala Indian restaurant. Three times winner of the Time Out Best Vegetarian Restaurant award. The atmosphere is relaxed with classic Indian music in the background. Dishes that don't seem vegan can be veganized.

Starters £1.50 to £3.00 such as banana boli with plaintain slices in a batter of rice and chickpea flour, seasoned with black sesame seeds and served with peanut and ginger sauce; medhu vadai spongy urad bean and chilli dumpling. Two soups such as peppery lentil broth with garlic, tomatoes, spices and tamarind.

Main courses feature a large dosa (stuffed pancake) selection and over nine curries from £5.00. There are side dishes like Kerala salad £4.00 of guava, avocadoes, stir-fried Indian shallots, fresh coconut, lemon juice and chilli powder; vendakka thoran of fresh okra fried with shallots, garlic, chillis, mustard seeds and curry leaves £3.25; kovakka olathiathu with tindori (like baby cucumbers), cashew nuts dry roasted with coconut mustard seeds and curry leaves £3.45. All kinds of rice such as fragrant lemon rice for £2.00.

Several desserts, some vegan, range from £2.25 and up.

Licensed for wine and beer. Extremely popular so booking about 2 days ahead is advisable.

Vegetarian Indian restaurant

55 Stoke Newington Church Street
Stoke Newington
London N16 0AR

Tel:020-7249 0344

Tube: Angel then 73 bus

Mon–Fri : 18.00–22.45,

Sat: 18.00–23.00

St. Paul's Vegetarian Organic Café

Veggie café in a church conversion, part of the Steiner School and adult education centre with arts and crafts. The interior is charming, retaining original features such as columns and arches with stone and wood carvings. They can get busy during term times. Seating outside weather permitting. Menus change daily. They usually have vegan options.

Starters include fresh foccacia bread, fried cashew nuts with lime and spring onions, marinated olives, and soup of the day from £1.00 to £2.25. Salads £1.50– £3.95.

3 main courses £2.65 to £4.95, two vegan, one wheat-free. For example chargrilled vegetables, alfafa, tomato & pesto sandwich on foccacia; dhal, rice and onion bhaji, potato and fennel rosti; or baked polenta with roast veg and tomato sauce.

Plenty of of vegan treats on the cake board such as apple crumble, date squares, chocolate and almond cake and banana, coffee and cashew cake.

Tea and coffee £1.00–£1.60. Soya milk always available. They are not licensed but they may allow you to bring your own with nominal corkage charge if they have enough interest to open in the evening.

Child portions and kids' menu Mon–Fri. All day breakfast on Saturdays.

Vegetarian café

Steiner School,
St Paul's Church,
1 St. Pauls Road,
(junction Essex Rd.)
Islington
London N1 2QH

Tel: 020–7359 3322

Tube: Angel,
then bus 38 or 73

or Highbury and
Islington then bus

Tues–Sat 10–16.00

Two Figs

Fabulous veggie café, deli and healthfood shop. Owners Andrea and Chris are great veggie/vegan cooks, so they get quite busy at lunchtimes. Eat in or take away.

Around 4 salads, usually pies or pastries, all made on the premises. The deli has a gourmet selection of olives and Sicilian patés. Filled rolls with some vegan options like red pepper and houmous, or veggie sausage and vegan mayo with salad. They make their own cakes, scones and muffins. Tuesday is vegan day when you can expect cakes like sticky coffee, or coconut sponge. Plenty of herbal teas, coffees, and cold juices.

Organic bread and gluten-free ranges, organic baby food. Unusual and sometimes handmade cards , aromatherapy oils, candles, cruelty-free toiletries and toothpastes and small gift items like Faith in Nature travel packs for weekends away. Ecover refill service.

101 Newington Green
Stoke Newington
London N1

Tel: 020–7690–6811

Tube: Angel then 73 bus,
or Highbury & Islington and short walk

Mon –Fri :
8.30–19.00,

Sat 8.30–17.00

Higher Taste Vegetarian Patisserie

Turkish vegetarian patisserie and café, possibly the only one in London, with seating for around fifteen people.

Vegetables stews, home-made houmous and other hot and cold dishes available.

They have lots of veggie Turkish delicacies such as savoury and sweet pastries with many fillings like potato and spinach, various cakes and Turkish style biscuits. Amazing baklavas, Turkish sweets with pistachio nuts and syrup, which have to be tasted to be believed, including honeyless ones for vegans.

Tea and coffee as well as cold drinks.

Vegetarian Turkish patisserie & café

47 Newington Green
Stoke Newington
Islington
London N16 9PX

Tel: 020-7359-2338

Tube:
Highbury & Islington then 73 to Newington Green

Open:
10am –till about 21.00 may vary

Clissold Park Café

Large café that used to be completely vegetarian but is now omnivorous. Situated in attractive grade 2 listed building in a park overlooking a lake, with outside seating around the lawn and underneath the portico. Within the 54 acre park are a children's play area and lido in summer.

Vegetarian snacks include veggie sausage and chips, pastries, pies and various sandwiches, although vegans may find it difficult to find anything. Cold drinks, coffee, herbal teas.

Omnivorous café

*Clissold Park
Stoke Newington
Church St
Stoke Newington
London N16*

Tel: 020–7249 0672

*Tube: Manor House,
Stoke Newington BR,*

bus 73,

*Highbury &
Islington then 20
minute walk*

*Open:
Varies according to
park opening hours
and the seasons*

The Cooler

Continental delicatessen, with an omnivorous smallish café at the back with seating for 15, in the heart of fashionable Stoke Newington. Although not veggie they have many veggie and vegan items.

The deli stocks a huge number of unusual ranges, such as continental sauces, condiments, breads, tofu, veggie sausages, burgers, patés and spreads. Also a small range of organic fruit and veg.

Approximately half the dishes in the café are veggie, including salads, sandwiches and pastries from £2.00 to £2.85. Desserts and cakes though not a lot for vegans.

The café closes at 6pm most evenings and 5pm on Sundays.

Continental deli & omnivorous café.

67 Stoke Newington Church Street
Stoke Newington
London N16 OAR

Tel: 020-7275-7266

Tube: Angel then 73 bus or Stoke Newington BR

Mon–Fri :
9.00–20.30 ,

Sat: 9.00–20.00,

Sun: 9.00–17.00

Fresh and Wild

Newly opened health food shop and café concentrating on organic produce. Offering a large range of veggie and vegan food, although they do sell a small amount of meat and fish.

The café seats around 15 people and serves until about ten minutes before the store closes. Serve-yourself salad bar, deli section with hot food, and another section dedicated to cakes where you buy coffee, soyacinno and tea. Cake ingredients are clearly labelled and usually one is vegan.

Big selection of organic fruit and veg as well as organic herb plants, organic wine, beers and ciders with clear veggie/vegan signs.

Another area is given over to all kinds of toiletries, aromatherapy oils, supplements and herbal remedies, many of which are veggie and vegan. There is usually a staff member who can advise you, and a nearby info board displays local alternative health practitioners.

Well stocked range of books on many subjects adjacent to the toiletries counter. There is a small bulletin board at the front of the shop for local events.

Health food shop & café

Stoke Newington Church Street Stoke Newington London N16 0LU

Tel: 020-7254-2332

Tube: Angel then 73 Bus

Mon–Fri : 9.00–21.00,

Sat: 8.30–20.30,

Sun: 10.00–20.00

Food For All

Popular veggie wholefood shop with complementary medicine, herbs and spices. Over 300 brands of herbal remedies, and dried herbs sold by weight. Great chilled section with many vegan cheeses and sausages. Take-away has latkas, samosas, falafels, kebabs, pakoras. There is a noticeboard in the shop and a yoga centre upstairs. Run by the Ananda Marga charity who are involved in a lot of work helping communities and rural areas become more prosperous.

Mother Earth Organic Market

Colourful wholefood shop with small amount of fresh organic fruit and veg, macrobiotic and organic products. They also sell veggie sausages, bread, pulses, grains and assorted veggie snacks including some vegan cakes and pies. The freezer counter has vegan ice-cream, choc ices and fruit ice-lollies in various flavours. Cruelty-free toiletries such as shampoos, lip balms, soaps and veggie toothpaste, green/environmental magazines, small selection of books, Ecover refills. Water purifying service available.

Vegetarian wholefood store

3 Cazenove Road
Stoke Newington
London N16 6PA

Tel: 020-8806 4138

Mon–Fri :
9.00–18.00,

Sat: 9.00–17.00,

Sun: 10.00–14.00

Wholefoods shop

5 Albion Parade
Albion Road
Stoke Newington
London N16 9LD

Tel: 020-7275 9099

Tube: Highbury and Islington or Angel then 73 bus

Mon–Fri:
9.30–20.00,

Sat: 9.30–19.00,

Sun: 11.00–19.00

Outer London
Camden

Places in Camden

Vegetarian restaurants

Omnivorous restaurants

Wholefood shops

CAMDEN

Cafe Seventy Nine

Modern vegetarian café and take-away with a small number of seats outside in one of London's most picturesque streets on the edge of Primrose Hill. Catering for the lunchtime and weekend trade predominantly. There is an extensive menu, though vegans will find almost all of the dishes contain dairy or eggs.

All day full English cooked breakfast £3.45–£5.75 depending how many items you go for. Croissants, bagels and toast £1.35–1.95.

Organic soup of the day with organic Neal's Yard roll £3.95. Houmous and warm wholemal pitta £3.25. Veggie burger and salad £4.25. Baked potato £2.25, or £3.35 with a filling then £1 per extra filling. Side salads £1.95. Sandwiches, toasted sandwiches, baguettes and bagels from £2.10.

Main courses such as pasta with pesto, pine nuts, cherry tomatoes and green salad £5.45. Bagel burger and deep fried new potatoes £5.75. Various giant salads £5.95.

Nine kinds of cakes and desserts £1.95–3.75.

Lots of teas, coffees and soft drinks, with a pot of tea for one £1.35 or for two £1.95. Freshly squeezed orange juice £2.25. Milkshakes £2.45 can be made with soya milk. Free corkage.

79 Regents Park Road
London NW1 8UY

Tel:
020–7586 8012

Tube: Chalk Farm

Open Mon–Sat 8.30–18.30,

Sun: 9.00–18.30

CAMDEN Vegetarian restaurants

Manna Vegetarian Restaurant

Vegetarian restaurant

4 Erskine Road
Primrose Hill
Hampstead
London NW3 3AJ

Tel: 020-7722 8028

Tube: Chalk Farm

Open Mon–Fri
18.30–23.00

Sat– Sun:
12.30–15.00 &
18.30–23.00

Very classy international gourmet vegetarian restaurant with lots of vegan food, set in a picturesque street near Primrose Hill, still going strong after 30 years, with incredibly friendly and efficient service by staff from all over the world. There is some seating in the conservatory and outside. The menu is constantly changing with the seasons.

Starters, around £5.50, include organic fritata; tempura of artichoke, aspargus and mangetout with tomato mayo at £6.25.

3 salads or you can go fo the Manna Meze of any 3 starters or salads for £13.75.

7 mains of which 6 are or have vegan options £8.95–£11.95. For example popadum stacks triple layered with vegetables and tamarind sauce £11.50; Indonesian coconut and cumin pancakes with tempeh, broccoli curry, red onion salad and coconut sambal £10.50.

Desserts £2.95 to £5.95, plenty vegan, like petits fours, a plate of truffles, chocolates and biscuits. Summer pudding stuffed with fresh berries served with cranberry and vodka sorbet. Vegan ice cream.

Special early evening deal 2 courses for £12.50 6.30pm–7.30pm.

Manna *(continued)*

Lots of liqueurs and vegan wines. Beer from £2.60, wine £2.95 a glass or £10.50 a bottle.

Kosher wine and food no problem. They even use organic soya.

They serve till 11pm and it's advisable to book as not surprisingly they are very popular.

The Ha Ha Veggie Stall

Stall selling falafels, drinks and large, homemade veggie burgers with a range of toppings such as avocado and pineapple. All are vegan except the cheeseburger. Prices £2-3.00.

Vegetarian & vegan take away

Row of food stalls, West Yard entrance Camden Lock market Camden Town London NW1

Tube: Camden Town

10-17.00 Sat and Sun

Organic Juice Bar

Friendly, all-vegan drinks stall selling a range of freshly-squeezed organic fruit and vegetable juices and lovely foamy sesame and banana based 'mylk' shakes. Prices from £2 to £4.

Vegan drink stall

West Yard Camden Lock Market Camden Town London NW1

Tube: Camden Town

Open Sat and Sun 10-17.00

Le Mignon

Sweet little Lebanese restaurant with a couple of outside tables on a quiet side street off Camden High St, round the back of Woolworths.

Like virtually all Lebanese places, main dishes are meat based and starters are vegetable based. Dairy products and eggs are rarely used. Staff are very friendly and it is clear from the menu what is veggie/vegan and what isn't.

There are around 12 vegan starters, so if you and a friend order 3 different ones each, you can create a tasty feast for little more than a tenner each.

Wagamama

Omnivorous fast food Japanese noodle bar with over nine veggie and vegan dishes. See Bloomsbury, WC1 branch for menu.

**Omnivorous
Libanese**

*9a Delancey Street
Camden Town
London NW1*

*Tel:
020–7387 0600*

*Tube:
Camden Town*

*Tue–Sun:
12.00 or 12.30–
23.30 or 24.00,*

closed Mon

**Omnivorous
Japanese**

*11 Jamestown Road
Camden Town
London NW1 7BW*

Tel: 020–74280800

*Tube:
Camden Town*

*Mon–Sat:
11.00–23.00,*

*Sun:
12.30–22.30*

Lemon Grass

Small, brightly lit and smoke-free Cambodian restaurant round the corner from Camden Road rail station.

All main meals are stir-fries and the menu makes them look a bit bland, but they are expertly cooked and suprisingly full of flavour. As they are prepared to order, you can customise them slightly by having vegetables added or left out.

The asparagus stir-fry is made with butter, but the other vegetable dishes were vegan at the time of visiting.

*243 Royal College Street
Camden Town
London NW1*

Tel: 020-7284 1116

*Tube:
Camden Town,
Camden Road BR*

*Open Every day
18.30–23.00*

Last orders 22.30

CAMDEN

Omnivorous restaurants

Fresh & Wild

Huge organic supermarket with a café which seats about fifteen people inside and has four tables outside.

The store sells everything from tea to toothpaste and has a take-away food and juice bar.

Muffins and cakes, some of them vegan, and soyacinno for vegan coffee lovers.

Large range of vegetarian and vegan products, the only meat is hidden in a fridge at the back. Great choice of organic fruit and vegetables.

Load up here for a day out in Regents Park or a wander to nearby fashionable Camden Lock market.

Organic supermarket

49 Parkway
Camden Town
London NW1 7PN

Tel: 020-7428 7575

Tube: Camden Town

Mon-Fri:
8.00-21.00,

Sat: 9.30-21.00,

Sun: 11.00-20.00

CAMDEN Wholefood & health food shops

Holland & Barrett

One of the largest London branches of this national chain. They have lots of take-away items like sandwiches, pies, pastries, Mexican slices and cakes. Large range of soya milks, vegan chocolate, dried goods, ready meals, nut roasts, toiletries and supplements.

191-200 High St
Camden
London NW1 0LT

Tel: 020-7485-9477

Tube:
Camden Town

Mon-Thu:
9.30-17.30,

Fri-Sun:
10.30-18.30

Holland & Barrett

Health food shop

Health food shop. This one doesn't have a freezer cabinet so no vegan ice-cream here.

55 High St
St John's Wood
London NW8 7NL

Tel: 020-7586 5494

Tube: St Johns Wood

Mon-Sat:
9.00-17.30,

Sun closed

Paradise Foods

Health food shop that stocks a wide range of unusual veggie foods from all around the world. Great selection of herbs and spices, many of them fresh, also fresh fruit and veg delivered 2-3 times a week. They have a small range of gluten-free and sugar-free foods.

164 Kentish Town Road
Kentish Town
London NW5

Tel: 020-7284 3402

Tube: Kentish Town

Mon-Sat:
10.00-18.00,

Sun closed

Sesame Health Foods

Wholefood shop

Wholefoods and fresh foods. Take-away items include soups, salads, rice and vegetables, hot-pots, snacks, pasta, stir-fries, cakes. Organic fruit and veg. Bread comes from several different bakers. All you need for a summer picnic on nearby Primrose Hill.

128 Regents Park Road
London NW1

Tel: 020-7586 3779

Tube: Chalk Farm

Open:
Mon-Sat:
9.00-18.00,

Sun: 12.00-17.00

CAMDEN Wholefood & health food shops

North London

Places in North London

Vegetarian restaurants

Wholefood & Health Food shops

SASA

One of the newest of the many Chinese vegan eat-as-much-as-you-like buffet popping up all over London, specialising in fake meats and popular with veggies and non-veggies alike.

£5 lunch, £6 dinner, or £3 for a take-away box.

Choose from chow mein, rice, sweet and sour veg "pork" balls, soya chicken, fake beef, crispy seaweed, fried aubergine, spring rolls, tofu and many more.

Cash only.

**Chinese
vegan restaurant**

*271 Muswell Hill
Broadway,
Muswell Hill,
London N10*

*Tel:
020-8442 0558*

*Tube:
Highgate or East
Finchley then bus*

*Every day
12–23.00*

Blue Ginger

New South Indian vegetarian restaurant with dosas, uttapam, idlis, dal, rice etc. On Sunday there is an all you can eat buffet for £5.95, most of it vegan and very tasty.

House wine £6.50 bottle, £1.70 glass.

Smoking and no smoking sections.

Visa, MC.

Indian vegetarian
restaurant

*7 East Barnet Road
Barnet
Hertfordshire
EN4 8RR*

*Tel:
020-8364 8220*

*Train:
New Barnet*

*Mon–Sat
17.00–22.30*

*Sun 13.00–23.30
(buffet till 22.30)*

CTV

Thai, Chinese and Japanese vegan buffet restaurant. Mouthwatering eat-as-much-as-you-like buffet for £5.00, or £6.00 after 6pm. You can fill up on goodies such as chow mein, crispy aubergine, spring rolls, Singapore noodles, Thai curry rice, sweet and sour won ton, and black beans hot pot.

Take-out box £3.00. They are unlicensed but you can bring your own for a minimal corkage charge.

One of the numerous new Chinese vegan restaurants springing up all over London offering fantastic value for money, founded by entrepreneur Ken Wong, then run independently by people who attend the same Buddhist temple.

Asian vegan buffet

22 Golders Green Rd
Golders Green
London NW11 8LL

Tel: 020-8201 8001

Tube: Golders Green

Every day
12.00–22.00

The Greenhouse Café

**Vegetarian café
& take away**

*Unit 64/67
Market Hall
Wood Green
London N22*

Tel:020-8881 1471

*Tube: Turnpike Lane,
Wood Green*

*Mon-Sat:
9.30-18.00,*

Sun: 11-17.00

Vegetarian café, snack bar and take-away inside covered market hall in Wood Green Shopping Centre, with vegan owner.

Homemade soup with bread, pate and toast, various sandwiches £1.20-3.00. Salads 70p-£2.10. Savouries £1.80-2.80, many of these are vegan, such as sos roll with meat substitutes, fishless fishcakes, curries, pasta, pies, flans, pasties, chilli sin carne, stews, bean bakes.

Desserts 37p-£1.20 like homemade cakes and crumbles.Tea 35p, coffee 30p, soya milk no problem.

Special diet such as candida, diabetic etc. can be catered for. Separate smoking area. Cheques but no credit cards. Private functions. Attached to a health shop.

Mahavir Sweet Mart

**Vegetarian
Indian take-away**

*127c High Road
East Finchley
London N2 8AJ*

Tel: 020-8883-4595

Tube: East Finchley

*Tue-Sat:
11.00-20.30,
Sun: 10.30-18.30,
closed Mon*

Indian vegetarian take-away with bhajias, pakoras, garlic potatoes, curries, vegan puris and of course Indian sweets.

Fiction Vegetarian Restaurant

Vegetarian
British international

60 Crouch End Hill
Crouch End
London N8 8AG

Tel: 020–8340 3403

Tube: Finsbury Park
then bus W7 or
Archway and bus 41

Wed–Sun:
18.30–22.00,

Fri & Sat
18.30–10.30

This is the only totally vegetarian restaurant in Crouch End. British and international cuisine with fusions from the Mediterranean, Asia and North Africa. Modern interior on two levels and a secluded courtyard garden for al fresco dining.

Starters: Vegan soups like roasted spiced pumpkin or pea, parsley and mint at £3.95. Moroccan Ras-al-Hanout couscous with peppers, red onion and apricots £4.45.

Of the five mains £9.25–10.45 on the autumn/winter menu, 3 were vegan. Vietnamese com-chay with sweet potato, mange-tout, cauliflower and spinach in black bean, plum ginger and lemon-grass sauce with rice; roasted butternut squash filled with button mushrooms, baby potatoes with chives and chestnut & bay gravy; gamekeeper's pie with 'mock' duck. Side orders ranging £1.95 to £3.95 like roast garlic mash, mixed leaf salad.

Desserts £4.35 like Tart of Darkness sweet filo pastry with strawberries and vegan vanilla topping option; peach and apple crumble with brandy custard.

Extensive wine list, liqueurs and soft drinks, world beers and pear cider.

Reservations on Friday and Saturday recommended. Last orders 21.30.

Jai Krishna

Vegetarian South Indian and Gujarati restaurant not far from the 'Gunners' ground.

There is a wide range of veg and vegan starters such as pakoras, katchuri (lentils in puff pastry) for £1.80.

Mains such as dosas, 35 kinds of curry, £4.25. Thalis £6.50. Try the coconut and lemon rice, and you can get brown rice. They have lots of new dishes such as pumpkin curry £3.25.

The usual Indian desserts plus mango slice or mango pulp for £1.85.

Very good value and can get busy, so worth booking on Fri or Sat nights. Corkage 75p bottle of wine, 20p a bottle of beer, and there's an off license opposite.

Vegetarian
South Indian

*161 Stroud Green
Road
Finsbury Park
London N4 3PZ*

Tel: 020-7272 1680

*Tube: Finsbury Park,
Crouch Hill BR*

*Mon-Sat:
12-14.00 &
17.30-23.00,*

closed Sun

Popcorn in the Park

Vegan café in a quiet grove to the west of the road as you approach the sharp right hand bend before Alexandra Palace.

Set meal and drink for about £5-6. Four freshly prepared dishes from all around the world.

No cheques, no cappuccino, no cards, no cola, no crisps, no candy, no junk! Service can be slow as they are offering on-site training to voluntary staff. Once you understand all this it is a great place to linger. On Sundays there are lots of newspapers and sometimes jazz music.

Vegan café

*in the Grove
near Garden Centre
Alexandra Palace Pk.
London N22 4AY*

Tel: 020-8883-0720

*Tube: Wood Green
then bus W3,
Highgate then bus
134 or 43*

*Every day
10.00-16.30
varies with seasons*

Oshobasho Café

Vegetarian café, in the middle of ancient Highgate Wood, with a huge rose and wisteria enclosed garden and seating outside for 200. Oshobasho means "Heaven on Earth", and you'll find this a blissful, blossom filled place to dine. In the summer they have live instrumental jazz, classical and jazz singers. Global food.

Winter porridge with fresh fruit and raisins £3.75, or try a gigantic vegetarian grilled breakfast for £5 including sausages, grilled mushrooms and heaps more.

Lite bites like foccacia with aubergine and tomato, or soup of the day with bread basket.

Mains include a rice or pasta dish with salad, usually one is vegan, £5.80. These could be winter root veg stew or chickpea with coriander curry; ratatouille; penne pasta with tomato sauce.

Desserts include apple pie, pastries, carrot cake – at least one vegan.

All the usual teas plus selection of herbal ones, barley cup, coffee, soycinnos. Great winter warmers, hot mulled wine or hot chocolate with cognac. Whole Earth colas, lemonade, soda. Wine £2.50 glass, beer £2.20. Children's portions on request.

See picture >

Vegetarian café

Highgate Wood
Muswell Hill Road
Highgate
London N10 3JN

Tel: 020–8444 1505

Tube: Highgate

Every day except Mon, 8.30 till dusk, later in the summer

Oshobasho café

Oshobasho Café

Oshobasho Café

Vegetarian Cuisine

Highgate Wood
Muswell Hill Road
London N10 3JN
Tel: 0208-444 1505

Opening Times
8.30 - half an hour
before gates close

Tuesday - Sunday
and Bank Holidays.

Peking Palace

Lovely vegan Chinese restaurant in the centre of North London with a huge menu. The décor is modern, bright and clean with deep reds and ochre yellows and beautiful flower displays that give the restaurant a lavish feeling. Definitely a good place to visit with a party of friends or for that quiet romantic dinner.

There is an all-you-can-eat lunch buffet for £4.95 (not on Sundays).

Be prepared to be astounded by the a la carte menu which will take you several minutes to read, currently 83 options to relish!

18 appetizers £3.00 to £4.80 like grilled Peking dumpling; vegetarian satay; asparagus tempura; soya drum sticks or capital soya spare ribs. We had a selection of the starters and were delighted with fresh tasty ingredients and innovative presentations that definitely added to the appeal of the dishes. But be warned, portions are very generous so you may not have room for a main course.

Range of soups from £2.50 like spinach, tofu and soya chicken.

Second course could be crispy aromatic "duck" served with pancakes and hoi sin sauce for £6.00.

The main course menu is divided into seafood (yes it's completely veggie), soya

Vegan Chinese restaurant

669 Holloway Road
London N19 5SE

Tel:
020-7281-8989

Tube:
Archway,
or Holloway Road
and then bus

Mon–Sat:
12.00–15.00,
18. 00–23.00;

Sun: 18.00–23.00

www.
thepekingpalace.com

Peking Palace *(continued)*

meat, tofu dishes, and curries. Try the sizzling soya beef steak Peking style which is very filling for £5.00, fried soya fish in black bean sauce £4.80, or Kung Po soya king prawn for £5.00.

There is a choice of 14 soya meat dishes, for example crispy soya duck in fruity sauce, or deep-fried soya chicken with lemon sauce £4.50.

7 kinds of tofu dishes such as fried tofu with black bean sauce £4.00. 5 types of curry: mixed veg, prawn, chicken, lamb or beef at £4.00 to £5.00.

Veg side dishes like steamed asparagus with oyster sauce, or fried green pak choi, around £3.00 and up. Plenty of rice and noodles to choose from £1.70.

Desserts include several flavors of vegan ice-cream, toffee and banana with ice-cream, or rambutan stuffed with pineapple in lychee syrup. They also plan to offer deep fried ice-cream in a thin batter, prices from £2.20 up to £3.50.

No smoking. Bring your own wine. Most major credit cards accepted. They will cater for private parties, functions or weddings.

Queens Wood Weekend Café

Vegetarian café

42 Muswell Hill Road
Highgate Woods
Highgate
London N10 3JP

Tel:
020-8444-2604

Tube:
Highgate

10.00–17.30
weekends only

This hideaway veggie café, part of the Cue Environmental Centre in Highgate Wood, was once a woodkeeper's cottage. They aim to use organic ingredients from their garden whenever possible, and the electricity and lighting is supplied by a solar panel. You can eat on the veranda or sit inside.

Starters and appetisers £3.00 such as carrot and coriander soup with bread, peanut soup with spinach and sweet potato, olive or mushroom paté on toast, spicy Mexican bean paté.

Main dishes with salad £4.80–4.95 vary, but could include pasta bake, chickpea and broccoli curry, falafel with pitta bread, shepherd's pie, hot pot, or tortilla wrap. Some vegan options available.

Desserts include passion cake, banana cake, chocolate tart and apple crumble with custard.

Wine £2.20 a glass, beer £2.00.

The café is available for private hire and very popular for children's parties, with treasure or fairy hunts in the woods followed by lunch. Also available to hire for environmental group meetings or birthday parties for adults. Children and dog friendly, dogs get a bowl of water.

Rani Indian Vegetarian Restaurant

Vegetarian Gujarati
& South Indian

7 Long Lane
Finchley
London N3 2PR

Tel:
020-8349 4386

Tube:
Finchley Central

Mon–Sat:
18.00–22.00,

Sun 12.15–14.30

then 18.00–22.00

Home-style Gujarati cooking at the top of Long Lane. Rani won the Good Curry Guide Best Veggie Restaurant Award 2001. Vegan friendly as they don't use egg at all and only vegetable ghee.

4 cold and 11 hot Indian starters, 3 soups, and 2 appetisers £2.50–£3.20.

There are 11 main dishes such as rashia bean val sak mildly spiced with cinnamon, cloves, root ginger and coriander for £4.10; akhaa bhindi bateta fried ladies fingers (okra) delicately spiced and slow cooked with whole baby potatoes and onions at £4.80. Some dishes have an African influence such as akhaa ringal, Kenyan aubergine slit and pressed in spices, ground peanuts and fresh coriander and cooked with potato.

Excellent breads – the essential accompaniment to Gujarati food. Don't miss the mithi roti, a sweetened lentil mix with cardamon and saffron, parceled in unleavened dough, roasted in vegetable ghee, sprinkled with poppy seeds.

13 desserts all under £3, but only the fresh fruit salad is vegan.
House wine £1.80 glass, £9.70 bottle. Small beer £2.20, large £4.40.

Braille menu available.

Taboon Bakery

Kosher bakery with lots of veggie options to choose from. Take-away snacks including hot potato, mushroom or aubergine latkas, pizza and falafel. Some vegan snacks available but advisable to check which ones are parve (dairy free). There is also a small seating area.

Vegetarian café & take away

17 Russel Parade
Golders Green Road
Golders Green
London NW11 9NN

Tel: 020-8455-7451

Tube: Golders Green

Sun-Thu:
9.00am-midnight,

Fri 10.00-15.00,

Sat closed

W.A.R. We Are Raw

New, informal centre, promoting a vegan organic raw/living food diet and lifestyle, dedicated to a sustainable permaculture environment and ethical consuming. Created as a resource centre for people to meet and exchange views, buy publications and merchandise.

They sell fresh fruit juices, flax oil and hemp crackers. The centre offers short-term accommodation in London for raw fooders and fruitarians.

A comprehensive programme is planned of lectures, yoga, workshops and social events designed to heighten awareness and knowledge for those wishing to pursue a raw food lifestyle.

Organic raw food restaurant

Unit K4, Arena
Business Centre,
71 Ashfield Road
Harringay
London N4 1NY

Tel: 020-8800-4849

Tube: Manor House

Open: 18.15 til late

The Veggie House

Vegetarian café and take-away in a community arts centre.

Breakfast from 10am till noon, with a "big daddy's special" for £3.50, as well as separate portions of beans on toast, veggie sausage; scones with jam from £1.00.

The lunch menu starts with soup and bread £3.50; asparagus and mushroom fan £4.60; sweet potato and coconut stew with coucous (vegan) £4.80; pasta with roast bell pepper and rocket £4.75; Shepherds pie is also vegan £4.75.

Lots of salads, small £2.50, large £3.50.

Desserts £2.50, some of which are vegan, include banana cake and carrot cake.

Tea and herbal teas 60p, coffees around £1.50, soyacinnos when soya milk is available.

Jazz on a Sunday from 12–16.00. Great place to take little ones especially when the theatre in the building has a kids' show. Special meal deals for kiddies for £1.95.

Jacksons Lane
Community Centre
269a Archway Road
London N6 5AA

Tel: 020-8348 7666

Tube: Highgate

Mon–Sun:
10.00–21.00,

Jazz on Sun
12.00–16.00

NORTH LONDON Vegetarian restaurants

Ital and Vital Takeaway

Small take-away with Caribbean flavour. Some veggie options like pea soup or ackee, pea and tofu stew, and steamed vegetables.

Caribbean
take-away

134 High Road
Seven Sisters
London N15 6JN

Tel: 020-8211 7358

Tube: Seven Sisters

Mon-Fri: 10.00-20.30

Alternative Health Shop

Vegetarian healthfood shop with some take-away items like sandwiches, some are vegan. Also sell homeopathic supplies.

Health food shop

1369 High Road
Whetstone
London N20 9LN

Tel: 020-8445 2675

Tube: Totteridge and Whetstone then 15 minute walk

Mon-Sat: 9.00-18.00

B Green Health Food Plus

Wholefood shop with sandwiches and pasties take-away selection with vegan options and some cakes, supplements, cruelty-free toiletries.

Health food shop
& take away food

104-106 Ballards La.
London N3 2DN

Tel: 020-8343 1002

Mon-Sat:
9.30-17.30,

Bumblebee Wholefood Co-op

Three shops with a massive selection of wholefoods, health foods, organic produce, macrobiotic foods and a bakery which makes organic bread. Enormous selection of vegan and organic wines and beers, probably the biggest in London. Takeaway foods and lunches 11.30–15.00 and always at least four vegan options. Box scheme for organic fruit and veg and delivery service for other produce.

Wholefoods, health foods & macrobiotic shop

30, 32 and 33
Brecknock Road
London N7 6AA

Tel: 020-7607-1936

Mon–Sat:
9.00-18.30,

Thurs till 19.30

Tube: Kentish Town

Finchley Health Food Centre

Vegetarian take-away salads, sandwiches, pies and pasties, some of which are vegan. They have a fridge freezer section including vegan ice-cream. Some cruelty-free cosmetics, books and fresh organic fruit and veg.

Healthfood & take-away

745 High Road
London N12 0BP

Tel: 020-8445 8743

Mon–Sat:
9.00-18.00,

Sun closed

Wholefood & health food shops

Green House

Wholefood store with vegan and vegetarian take–away which includes pies, curries, fake meat dishes and soya products. You can buy nuts and pulses by weight. Their freezer is well stocked and includes vegan ice-cream, veggie sausages and burgers.

They also have a nearby veggie café in the covered market called The Greenhouse that uses the shop produce to make hot veggie and vegan dishes. (page 159)

Units 65–68, Wood Green Shopping Ctr. High Road Wood Green London N22

Tel: 020-8881 1471

Tube: Wood Green

Mon–Fri: 9.30–18.00,

Sun: 11.00–17.00

Just Natural

Organic food shop

Family run organic food shop, although not veggie. On the hill not far from Alexandra Palace, so good for picnic supplies. Organic foodstuffs including pastas, noodles, breads, fruit and veg. Organic baby foods, homeopathic remedies, veggie and vegan wines. Local box scheme for delivering organic veg.

They do daily fresh lunch take-always Mon–Fri such as Moroccan stew with dates, couscous and chickpeas, Tuscan salad with bread, Thai coconut & lentil soup, all £2.95 for small and £3.50 for a large carton. Veggie and sometimes vegan sandwiches, like houmous and salad, also veggie samosas.

304 Park Road Crouch End London N8 8LA

Tel: 020-8340 8669

Tube: Alexandra Palace

Mon–Sat: 9.00–19.00,

Sun: 11.00–15.00

Haelan Centre

Large independent wholefood shop located in hip Crouch End just down the hill from Fiction restaurant, with a complementary health clinic upstairs. They celebrated their 30th birthday in October 2001, making this one of the oldest wholefood centres in London. A great place to buy presents or just little cruelty-free luxuries to pamper yourself.

Ground floor is food, including organic fruit & veg, large fridge/ freezer section with several types of vegan cheese, ice-creams and selection of veggie foods. Well stocked fresh take-away food with vegan options, sushi, pancakes, pies and cakes. Herbs, teas, amazing amount of dry wholefoods and pulses and a good selection of seaweeds and oriental sauces.

The second floor is an Aladdin's cave of non-food items which always smells lovely thanks to the fab toiletries. There is a clinic with a counter which is usually staffed for those wanting to make appointments. Great variety of cruelty-free toiletries, oils, perfumes, soaps, lipsticks, moisturisers, and more cruelty-free shampoos than you've ever seen. Many household products, like environmentally friendly cleaning stuff and vegetable wash.

41 The Broadway
Crouch End
London N8 8DT

Tel: 020-8340 4258

Train: Crouch Hill, Hornsey

Mon-Thur, Sate 9.00-18.00,

Fri 9.00-18.30,

Sun: 12.00-16.00

NORTH LONDON Wholefood & health food shops

Holland & Barrett

Health food store. Fresh take-away food delivered on a Monday like veggie pies, pastries and sandwiches. Vegan ice-cream.

Health food shop

452 Holloway Road
London N7 6QA

Tel: 020-7607 3933

Tube: Holloway

Mon-Sat: 9.00-17.30

Holland & Barrett

Fresh take-away snacks such as pies and soya sausage rolls, pastries, some vegan. Small chilled section but no freezer section. Also dried foods, seeds, supplements, egg-free mayo, and some toiletries.

Health food shop

121 Muswell Hill
Road
Muswell Hill
London N10 3HS

Tel: 020-8883-1154

Tube: Finsbury Park
then W7 bus

Mon-Sat: 9.00-17.30,

Holland & Barrett

National chain of healthfood stores, this shop has fridge and freezer section with veggie sausages and burgers.

Vegetarian &
vegan take away

81 Golders Green
Road
London NW11 8EN

Tel: 020-8455 5811

Tube: Golders Green

Mon-Sat: 9.30-18.00,
Sun: 10.00-16.00

Holland & Barrett

Usual health foods here. This shop has a freezer section with veggie burgers and sausages and sometimes vegan fishcakes.

Health food shop

129–131 High Street
Wood Green
London N22 6BB

Tel: 020-8889-4759

Tube: Wood Green

Mon–Sat: 9.00–17.30,
Sun: 10.00–16.00

Natural Health

Vegetarian wholefoods including vegan ice-creams, vegan cheeses and a take-away. Stocks gluten-free, vegan, and special diet ranges. Also homeopathic and herbal remedies, and cruelty-free cosmetics.

Vegetarian wholefoods

339 Ballard's Lane
London N12 8LJ

Tel: 020-8445 4397

Tube: Woodside Park, or W263 bus

Mon–Sat: 9.00–17.30,
Sun Closed

Pure Health

Wholefoods, cosmetics and vitamins. Some fresh take-away items, a few things are vegan, and they have a chilled section.

Wholefoods shop

56 Chaseside
Southgate
London N14 5PA

Tel: 020-8447-8071

Mon–Sat: 9.00–17.30,
Sun closed

Temple Health Foods

Vegan
drink stall

Lots of great take away food here, falafels, pasties, pies sandwiches, salads, many vegan. Two trained nutritionists on site so advice always available. They stock vitamins and minerals and they are happy to order anything for you.

17 Temple Fortune Parade
London NW11

Tel: 020-8458 6087

Mon-Fri:
9.00-18.00,

Sat: 9.00-17.30,

Sun: 10-14.00

Victoria Health Foods

Health food store

Great little health food store, with visiting food allergist every 6 weeks. The manageress Marianne is a nutrition consultant and can give advice.
Very well stocked with large fridge freezer section that has 3 varieties of vegan ice-cream. Plenty of choice for chocoholics also as they stock Boujabouja gourmet vegan chocs amongst their naughty but nice goodies.
Wide range of dry foodstuffs including wheat-free sections, fruit, nuts and seeds. Also huge range of herbal and homeo-pathic remedies and cruelty-free toiletries, toothpaste and household products.

99 Muswell Hill Broadway
Muswell Hill
London N10 3RS

Tel: 020-8444-2355

Tube: Finsbury Park, then W7 bus

Mon-Sat:
9.00-18.00,

Sun: 11.00-17.00

Wholefood Express

Wholefood shop

This wholefood shop has a community feel to it. As well as wholefood and organic products they stock lots of veggie/vegan snacks such as wraps, pastries, pies and samosas. The frozen counter also has veggie sausages, haggis, vegan cheese and ice-cream. Also Ecover re-fills, herbal and aromatherapy oils.

Organic fruit and veg box scheme for home deliveries on Thursday, but phone first on Wednesday for order confirmation.

95 Southgate Road
Hackney
London N1 3JS

Tel: 020–7354 4923

Mon–Sat:
10.00–19.00,

GNC (General Nutrition Centre)

Health foods
& take–away

Health food shop. Not exclusively vegetarian as some of their supplements contain gelatin but they don't stock meat products. Some fresh take–away food, usually some for vegans. Non–dairy chocolate and vegan ice-cream. Toiletries and household products.

243 The Broadway,
Muswell Hill N10

Tel: 020–8444 7717

Tube: Finsbury Park,
then W7 bus

Mon–Sat:
9.00–18.00,

Sun 12–17.00

NORTH LONDON   Wholefood & health food shops

North West

ces in Hampstead

NORTH WES

Vegetarian restaurants

International vegetarian

72 Belsize Lane
Belsize Park
London NW3 5BJ

Tel: 020-7435-7733

Tube: Belsize Park

Mon-Tues:
18.00-23.00,

Wed-Sun:
12.00-15.00 then
18.00-23.00

...ss veggie restaurant, this is the ...ster to the long established Gate ...urant in Hammersmith. Wood tables, ...rs and floor plus subdued lighting add ...o the minimalist yet opulent feel. Modern international cuisine.

Starters £3.50 to £6.25 include vegan soup of the day, mushroom bruschetta, antipasto sandwich filled with roasted veg, or Mediterranean salad.

Main courses include vegan Mussaman curry £11.25, a fragrant combination of cumin, star anise, lime cinnamon, baby corn, new potatoes and mange tout, served with lemon grass rice and salsa; porcini polenta tart, pan fried on a bed of sautéed radicchio and roast peppers finished with ratatouille.

Lots of side orders like creamy potato and parsnip mash or rocket and sweet potato salad, £3.25 up to £4.50.

Several desserts including chocolate mud cake at £5.50, hummingbird cake with passion fruit coulis (vegan) £5.00, various ice-creams and sorbets, some vegan.

Extensive wine list with veggie and vegan ones clearly labelled.

We recommend you reserve on a Friday or Saturday evening. All major cards accepted. Smoke free.

VitaOrganic

New 100% vegan Oriental organic restaurant with a self-serve buffet for £5.90 before 6pm and then £6.90. The place has a really nice atmosphere with Chinese lanterns, bamboo, friendly staff and a vegan proprietor. Organic produce is used wherever possible and no MSG. A lot of thought has been put into the menu, which is constantly evolving. It is especially ideal for those on a wheat free, food combining, or macrobiotic diet.

The buffet includes Malaysian, Thai, Chinese and Japanese dishes such as seaweed soup, teriyaki, Malaysian tempura, Chinese five spice, Thai curry, Malaysian curry. Both brown and white rice, millet and vegetables, stir-fry, plus salad bar

Also a la carte with Japanese food too like sushi, from £2.50 to £12. As we go to print, they are opening a sushi and noodle bar with their own sushi chef. Sushi from £2 to £12. All kinds of noodles from all parts of Asia, such as Vietnamese, Malaysian, Pad Thai, organic soba noodles, udon.

For dessert you could have a small firm jelly dessert made of apple and agar-agar or a sticky rice pudding.

Soft drinks £1.50 each and there is organic wine. They plan to open a juice bar in the future.

279c Finchley Rd
West Hampstead
London NW3 6ND

Tel:
020-7435 2188

Tube: Finchley Road;
BR Finchley Road and
Frognal

Mon–Sun:
12 noon to 11pm

NORTH WEST LONDON Vegetarian restaurants

riendly Falafels

Since 1989, falafel stall in front of the House of Mistry health food shop next to Hampstead Heath.

Falafel £3.40, with hummous £3.90. Salad in pitta £2.50, or with hummous too. 6 falafel balls £1.50. Also Whole Earth cola, lemonade, tea, coffee.

in front of House of Mistry shop,
15–17 South End Rd
Hampstead
London NW3

Wed–Sat 19.30–
24.00
Sun 13.30–24.00
Train:
Hampstead Heath

Hampstead Health Food Shop

Vegan & veggie health foods & take–away shop

Health foods and a wide selection of take–away, some organic, with lots of vegan options including cottage pies, veggie sausages, rice and curry, cakes and flapjacks. Organic dried fruit, nuts and seeds. They stock the complete Ecover range and also have green cosmetics.

57 Hampstead High
Street
London NW3 1QH

Tel: 020-7435 6418
Tube: Hampstead
Mon–Sat 10–18.00,
Sun: 12.00–17.00

Holland & Barrett

Health food shop

Usual range of health and wholefoods. Omnivorous fast food Japanese noodle bar with over nine veggie and vegan dishes. See Bloomsbury, WC1 branch for menu.

14 Northways Parade
Swiss Cottage
London NW3 5EN

Tel: 020-7722 5920
Tube: Swiss Cottage
Mon–Sat 9.00–17.30,
Sun closed

House of Mistry

Health food shop owned by Mr Mistry, a renowned vegetarian chemist and nutritionist who is currently producing organic products such as insect repellent for plants and humans, and recently won the Indian equivalent of an M.B.E. for his outstanding achievements in chemistry. He has a catalogue of products which are available by mail order worldwide. There is also a clinic attached for advice on healing. Cosmetics, body products, oils and toiletries, all of which are definitely not tested on animals.

Health food shop

*15–17 South End Rd
Hampstead
London NW3*

Tel: 020-7794 0848

*Tube: Belsize Park,or
Hampstead Heath BR*

*Mon–Fri:
9.00–19.00,*

Sat : 9.00–18.00,

Sun closed

Peppercorn's Organic & Natural Healthfoods

All the standard wholefood shop items plus a whopping selection of take-away food and macrobiotic specialities from around the world. Mexican bean slices, vegetarian rotis, country pies, vegetarian sushi, spinach filo pastries, tofu parcels, rice rolls, organic hummous. Vegan and wheat free cakes.

**Health foods &
take-away shop**

*193-195 West End
Lane
West Hampstead
London NW6 1RD*

Tel: 020-7328 6874

*Tube:
West Hampstead*

*Mon-Sat:
10.00-19.00,*

Sun closed

Places in
Willesden & Kilburn

Vegetarian restaurants

Omnivorous restaurants

Wholefood shops

Bhavna Sweet Mart

Indian vegetarian and vegan take-away sweets, curries for under £2, naan, parathas, bhajias etc.

Don't get there too late in the day in case all the best stuff's been scoffed, or reserve some food by phone.

They are also open on Christmas Day if you feel like something different!

237 High Road
Willesden
London NW10

Tel: 020-8459 2516

Tube:
Willesden Green,
Dollis Hill

Open every day
10.00-21.00

NORTH WEST LONDON Vegetarian restaurants

Sabras Indian Vegetarian Restaurant

Family-run vegetarian and 75% organic South Indian and Gujarati restaurant, with some North Indian dishes too. Around 50 items on the huge menu, almost all of them vegan and they can cater for wheat-free and Jains. They specialise in the use of ground nut oil, fresh ginger, chilli, garlic, lemon, coconut and coriander.

7 starters, all vegan, £3.25-3.50, such as bhel puri, sev puri, pani puri, samosas, chana dal steam cooked, fried banana balls.

10 kinds of dosa £3.50-7.50, or have a small one as a starter. These are south Indian pancakes filled with vegetables and spices and make a complete meal. All kinds of Indian vegetable and lentil dishes £4.95-5.50 like sweet potato, Kashmiri kofta, spinach palak with spices, steamed chick pea and potato with ginger, mixed lentils and beans. Fill up with thin chapatis or thick paratha bread, which can be stuffed with vegetables.

Two of the four desserts are vegan, either chilled mango pulp or puran-poli, a mini chupati filled with sweetened Toover dal, enriched with nutmeg, cloves and cardamon, £3.50.

Two page drinks menu including house wine £2.50 glass, £10 botle. Beer £3. Coffee or pot of tea £1.75. Smoking tables available but no pipes or cigars. Visa, MC, Amex, Diners. 12.5% service charge.

South Indian Gujarati restaurant

263 High Road
Willesden Green
Willesden Green
London NW10 2RX

Tel: 020-8459-0340

Tube: Willesden Green, Dollis Hill. Close to Willesden bus garage.

Tue-Sun: 18.30-23.30, last orders 22.30,

closed Mon

Willesden Sweet Mart

Vegetarian Indian meals and snacks to take away with a few seats to eat in. This is mainly a sweet mart and all the delicacies are veggie but you'll need to ask which ones are vegan.

They also have a resturant in Wembley, Middlesex, called Chetna's.

265 High Road
Willesden
London NW10 2RX

Tel: 020-8451 1276

Tube: Dollis Hill

Wed–Mon:
10.00–20.00,

Sat–Sun from 9.30.
Closed Tue.

Foodworld

Take away
& wholefoods

Lots of vegan and middle-eastern food and toiletries, bulk legumes, lavah bread, nuts and seeds. Small organic and take-away section and some fresh herbs.

244 Kilburn High
Road
London NW6 2BS

Tel: 020-8328 1709

Tube: Kilburn

Mon–Sat:
9.30–20.30,

Sun: 10.30–18.30

Hugo's Restaurant

Organic omnivorous restaurant. 50% veggie global menu using fresh seasonal produce. They don't use any animal fat in cooking or preparation of food. Some of the veggie options may be vegan, but we advise vegans to check by phone first as the menu differs every day.

They offer a full English veggie (can be vegan) breakfast for £6.80, or pancake with maple syrup and/or fruit salad.

Lunch served from 12.30–16.00 with daily special on the board, £2–£12, e.g. veg stir fry with brown rice £7.80, herb risotto £7.80, big soup £4.50. The evening menu has a set platter for veggies which included a starter of wild mushroom risotto with truffle oil for £6.80. The main course £11.80 was either chilli tofu with tempura of vegetables and quinoa with sesame dressing; or courgette timbale with roast beetroot, braised fennel and walnut oil with balsamic vinaigrette. Various side dishes at £3.80 each.

Desserts £5.50 and cakes £2–£4.50 such as vegan chocolate or lemon polenta.

House wine £2.80 glass, £9.80 bottle.

Previously called The Organic Café until November 2001.

25 Lonsdale Road
Queens Park
London NW6 6NN

Tel:
020–7428–7575

Tube:
Queen's Park

Mon Sat:
9.30–23.00

NORTH WEST LONDON

Omnivorous restaurants

Human Nature

Health food store where the take-away selection has an Eastern slant, and they stock most other veggie foods and household products and toiletries. The manager, Mr Nari Sadhuram, the manager, sells veggie remedies for various maladies such as jet-lag and hangovers, and is also a trained masseur so you can have a Swedish or an Indian head massage or make an appointment for a home visit.

Health food store & take-away

25 Malvern Road
London NW6

Tel: 020-7328 5452

Mon-Fri:
9.00-18.00,

Sat: 9.00-17.00,

Sun closed

Meeras Health Food Centre

Heath food shop with vitamins and supplements and also a freezer section. Free advice on products. No fresh take-away but they have dried fruits, nuts and seeds.

Health food shop

2 High Street
Harlesden
London NW10 4LX

Tel: 020-8965 7610

Mon-Sat:
10.00-18.00,

Sun closed

Mistry Health Food Shop & Pharmacy

Health food shop

Health food shop with pharmacy and two homeopaths next door. Take-away food includes sandwiches, salads, samosas, burgers etc. with lots for vegans. Reflexology, optician, acupuncture and massage offered.

16–20 Station Parade
Willesden Green
London NW2 4NH

Tel: 020-8450 7002

Tube: Willesden Grn.

Mon –Sat: 9.00–19.00

Olive Tree

Vegetarian
wholefood shop

Vegetarian wholefood shop with lots of snacks for veggies and vegans. Loose herbs, flower remedies, vitamins and supplements. Take-away selection includes rolls and sandwiches and some meals. Large selection of fresh organic fruit and veg. All displayed in a charming old worldly style wooden interior.

84 Willesden Lane
London NW6 7TA

Tel: 020-7328 9078

Mon–Sat: 10.00–18.30
Wed: 13.00–18.30,

Revital Health Shop

Health food shop

Fridge and freezer section, take-away food includes pies and pasties, many of them vegan. Lots of vitamins and minerals and the nutritionist on site gives free advice on supplements. Mail order with freephone number 0800-252875.

35 High Road
Willesden NW10

Tel: 020-8459-3382

Tube: Willesden
Green

Mon–Fri: 9.30–19.00,
Sun: 11.00–16.00

Places in Hendon

Vegetarian restaurants

Wholefood shops

Rajen's Vegetarian Restaurant

Indian restaurant
& take away

Excellent value Indian vegetarian restaurant and take-away close to the mega-crossroads where the M1 meets the North Circular meets the Edgware Road. Don't miss their speciality eat as much as you like buffet thali £5 till 3pm, £6.50 evenings and all weekend.

Also an a la carte menu with lots of fast food items like bhel poori, kachori, masala dosa, onion uttapam, idli, spring roll.

Soft drinks only. Free car park at the back.

*195–197 The Broadway
West Hendon
London NW9 6LP*

Tel: 020-8203 8522

Tube: Hendon BR

*Open Every day
11.00–22.00*

Chandni Sweet Mart

Indian vegetarian
take-away

Indian vegetarian take-away offering samosas, bhajias, but mostly sweets such as jelabi, barfi, ladu, some of them vegan as they use vegetable ghee.

*141 The Broadway
West Hendon
London NW9 7DY*

Tel: 020-8202 9625

*Tube:
Hendon Central*

*Every day:
9.00–18.00,*

Sun: 9.00–17.00

Kai

Chinese vegan buffet restaurant where you can eat as much as you like for just £5. Scoff till you drop from boiled and stir-fried rice, spring rolls, tofu, stir-fry veg, soya meats and noodles.

If there's food left from lunch then they reload the platters and stay open in the afternoon.

Drinks £1–£2.50, no alcohol but you can bring your own and pay 50p corkage. Seating for 50 people.

244 The Broadway
West Hendon
London NW9 6AG

Tel: 020-8203-6925

Tube: West Hendon

Mon–Sat:
12.30–22.30,

Sun 17.00–22.00

NORTH WEST LONDON

Vegetarian restaurants

Hendon Healthfood Centre

Health food shop with a selection of organic bread, some take-away items like sandwiches, samosas and veggie carrot cake. The chiller section has the Tival range of veggie products and two vegan ice-creams.

125 Brent Street
Hendon
London NW4

Tel: 020-8202 9165

Tube: Hendon

Mon–Fri:
9.00–18.00,
Sat: 10.00–14.00.

Sun closed

Holland & Barrett

Health food shop

Health food store that is part of a long established group all over the UK. This one is open quite late to accommodate Brent Cross shoppers.

Unit W16
Shopping Centre
Brent Cross
London NW4 3FP

Tel: 020-8202 8669

Tube: Brent Cross

Mon–Fri:
9.00–20.00,

Sat: 9.00–19.00,

Sun: 11.00–17.00

NORTH WEST LONDON Wholefood & health food shops

Places in Kingsbury & Edgware

Vegetarian restaurants

Wholefood shops

Chai

Almost entirely vegan Chinese restaurant, Buddhist owned. They specialize in an astonishing range of fake meats and lots of other dishes. The ideal night out for both reluctant and avid vegetarians, with 132 items on the menu which you can see in full on their website.

25 appetizers £2.50 to £5.00 like tempura, sesame toasts and seven kinds of soup.

You will be spoilt for choice with 23 main courses £3.50-4.00 such as broccoli, quick fried with garlic sauce; satay with chopped onions and peppers in peanut sauce; sea spiced aubergine; French beans in black bean sauce. Lots of tofu dishes like ginger tofu, kung po tofu (deep fried with chestnuts), ma po tofu diced with Szechuan cabbage, onions, ginger and chillis stir fried in a hot sauce. Or you could be tempted by the aromatic crispy veg-duck with pancakes with hot hoi sin sauce, cucumber and spring onion for £6.00. Lots of noodle and rice dishes too.

2 set meals £11.50 or £13.95 per person.

Free birthday meal for a party of six or more, so the birthday person eats free, plus a free photo. Advance booking required for this and not on Fri or Sat.

There's a table with books on vegetarianism and Buddhist philosophy. Free delivery within a three mile radius.

236 Station Road
Edgware
Middlesex HA8 7AU

Tel:
020-8905 3033

Tube:
Edgware

Mon-Fri :
12.00-14.30 and
18.00-23.30,

Sat: 12.00-15.30
and 18.30-23.30,

Sun: 12.00-23.30

www.chai-veg.co.uk

Visa, MC

N.B. The other
branch in Harrow is
now serving meat

NORTH WEST LONDON Vegetarian restaurants

Jays Pure

Vegetarian restaurant, take–away and juice bar with a great menu and so much choice. Fast food but healthy with Indian, Chinese, Mexican and Thai menus. They use sunflower oil in cooking so many dishes are suitable for vegans.

Snacks or starters from £1.25 up to £6.50 including the usual Indian favourites and others, such as kachori (three piece turnover filled with dhal), corn bhaji, mogo chips, chilli mushroom, stir-fried aubergine or King Pow corn. There are also Thai dishes like Thai green curry, or Thai noodles priced at £3–£5.00.

Indian mains are all under £6.00 and include vegetable biriyiani and Hyderabad masala dosa.

Chinese curries such as baby corn with mushroom Szechuan style, aubergine black bean sauce, Manchurian cauliflower, all around £5.00.

The Mexican dishes are tortilla chips, tacos with chili bean and salad, burritos with picante sauce, Mexican rice and refried beans. These are £3 up to £6.00.

Indian desserts £3.60–5.00 but nothing vegan.

They also have 3 types of veggie burger and 7 types of noodles.

*547 Kingsbury Road
London NW9 9EL*

*Tel:
020-8204 1555*

*Open 365 days a
year 12.30–23.00*

NORTH WEST LONDON

Vegetarian restaurants

Gayatri Sweet Mart

Indian vegetarian take-away. 46 dishes £7-£8 per kilo. Savouries like samosa 45p, bhajias, dhokra, kachori.

Sweets include barfis, pendas, ladoos, chevda (Bombay mix).

467 Kingsbury Road
Kingsbury
London NW9 9DY

Tel: 020-8206 1677

Mon-Fri :
10.30-18.30,

Sat 10-19.00,

Sun 9-16.00

Satyam Sweet Mart

Vegetarian Indian sweet shop with take-away snacks only such as samosas and bhajias.

24 Queensbury
Station Parade
Edgware
Middlesex HA8

Tel:
020-8952 3947

Tube:
Queensbury

Mon-Sat:
10:00-19.00,
Sun: 9.00-18.00

Yogi Ji's Café

Busy and fun vegetarian café and juice bar that promotes the health benefits of being veggie and claims to have the 'ultimate falafel experience'. They don't use eggs in any of their patisserie so many snacks are suitable for vegans such as the pancakes.

Breakfast served 8am–11am consisting of an egg-free Spanish omelette, sweet pancakes, veggie soya hot dog and bacon, plus cereals and freshly baked baguettes.

Spring rolls, samosas, taco chips, cassava tempura, herb bread and mushroom tempura, £1.50 to £3.99 depending on eat-in or take-away. Salads £2.75 out, £3.75 in.

Five types of veggie burger £2.49 or £3.49. Falafel £2.99–£4.99.

Toasted sandwiches and Mexican style wraps like bean burrito or enchiladas for £3.99–£4.99.

Fruit cocktails such as orange, sugar cane and soda, passion soda water and lemonade, all around £2.50.

Egg-free pancakes and hot apple pie for afters £2.75 to £3.99.

The café has a kids fun room with clay and T-shirt painting and is also available for private parties.

658 Kingsbury Road, nr Kingsbury Roundabout London NW9 9HN

Tel: 020-8204-6204

Mon–Sun 8am–midnight

NORTH WEST LONDON

Vegetarian restaurants

Diet & Health Centre

Health food store. No fresh take-away here but they do have a good freezer section with frozen meals. Also a range of cruelty-free toiletries.

28 Watling Avenue
Burnt Oak
Edgware
Middlesex HA8

Tel: 020-8952-9629

Tube: Burnt Oak

Mon-Sat:
9.00-17.30,

Sun closed

NORTH WEST LONDON Wholefood & health food shops

Outer London
The East End

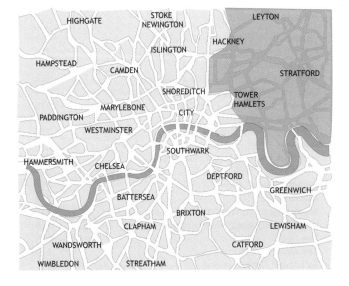

Places in the East End

Vegetarian restaurants

Wholefood shops

Gallery Café

Cosmopolitan vegetarian café run as a co-operative by Buddhists with an international menu. Outside umbrella seating in summer on the flower filled south facing terrace.

A different home made soup each day £2.10. Turkish meze or filled bagels £1.30–£1.90. Toasted ciabatta and focaccia also available. Three salads each £1.50. Dish of the day £3.50 or £4.20 could be Spanish tortilla, casserole or stew, or pasta, sometimes vegan.

Home made pastries and cakes, a few of them vegan with vegan cream. Juices, tea, coffee and soya milk is usually available. Alcohol free, like the people who run the place. Smoking outside only. Cheques and most cards accepted on orders over £5.

Vegetarian café & restaurant

21 Old Ford Road
Bethnal Green
London E2 9PL

Tel: 020–8983-3624

Tube: Bethnal Green, then short walk

Mon,Wed–Sat: 10.30–17.00,

Tues: 12–17.00,

Sun closed

Chawalla

New Indian vegetarian restaurant with South Indian, Gujarati and Punjabi food. Really good and vegan friendly. Eat for around £6 a head. Some unusual dishes such as spicy masala potato chips gardished with lime juice, cassava chips with tamarind sauce, lentil and rice pancakes. No smoking. No alcohol. Visa, MC over £5.

Green Street is becoming like a more multicultural Southall or Brick Lane, full of Asian shops run by Sikhs, Muslims, Hindus, Buddhists, even Hare Krishnas, selling henna, incense, clothes and with several restaurants.

Indian vegetarian restaurant

270 Green Street
Forest Gate
London E7 8LF

Tel: 020–8470 3535

Tube: Upton Park

Every day
11.00–21.00

Gannets Café

Vegetarian café in a not-for-profit community owned environmental centre. Dishes from around the world change daily and the head chef is vegan so you can expect some delicious vegan treats. Some seating outside in the summer.

Starters £2.20–3.75 such as Mediterranean black bean and olive soup, guacamole and blue tortilla chips. Salads 60p per portion like puy lentil with veg, vegan coleslaw, smoked tofu or couscous.

3-5 veggie main courses daily from £3.75 such as flageolet bean casserole with roast garlic cream topping and herb crust, or roast veg with houmous and red pepper in a puff pastry – both vegan. Main courses come with a choice of salads or roast/hot veg in the winter or evenings.

Several of the desserts are vegan like baked lemon and ginger cheesecake, almond and banana cake, blackberry fruit crumble, vegan ice-cream, and chocolate cake.

Vegan organic wines and beers, tea, coffee soya milk always available.

Cheques with cheque card but no credit cards. Children portions on request (highchairs available). Available for private dinner parties. Outside catering from one cake to buffets or picnic food for 1,000.

Hornbeam Environmental Centre
458 Hoe Street
Walthamstow
London E17 9AH

Tel: 020-8558 6880

Tube: Walthamstow Central, Leyton Midland

Mon –Thurs: 12-15.30, 12-15.30 then 19.00–22.00,

Sat: 10-16.30,

Sun closed

EAST END

Vegetarian restaurants

Pumpkins

Vegetarian wholefood café–restaurant with a real Hackney feel to it, very popular with the locals and great value for money. Vegans are well catered for too. The seating area, with big floppy sofas, is great for lounging around – don't come in a suit.

Around 9 starters, over half vegan, such as garlic mushrooms.

The same number of main courses £3.95–4.95 like nut roast, lentil roast, vegan cheese pie, tofu burgers.

Salads and side dishes like roast potatoes or parsnip chips £1–1.75.

Vegan cakes and desserts start at around £1.20.

Pumpkins now do juices and vegan smoothies. Fair-trade coffees, tea and herbal teas. Bring your own booze for 40p corkage, there's an off-license a few doors down.

Parties of six and over should book.

Vegan & veggie restaurant

76a Clarence Road
Hackney
London E5 8HB

Tel: 020-8533-1214

Train: Hackney Central BR

Mon–Sat:
12.00–21.30,

closed Sun

EAST END Vegetarian restaurants

Ronak Restaurant

Vegetarian South Indian restaurant and take-away still going strong after over 20 years.
Masala dosa £4, thali with two curries £7.50. Lots of snacks like bhel puri, samosas, kachori.
At weekends they do a lot of outside catering so are usually closed, but if you ring first you may get lucky once a month. When open it's Sat-Sun 2-8pm, and on Sunday there is an eat-as-much-as-you-want buffet for £7.50 with five kinds of curries.

Sth. Indian restaurant & take-away

*317 Romford Road
Forest Gate
London E7 9HA*

Tel: 020-8519 2110

Tube: Stratford, Upton Park, Forest Gate BR

Tue-Fri: 12-21.00,

Sat-Sun sometimes open (phone first), closed Mon

Sakonis Vegetarian Restaurant

One of three London vegetarian Indian restaurants that also offer some Chinese dishes. For menu see Wembley, Middlesex, branch. (page 291)

Vegetarian Indian & Chinese

*149-153 Green Street
Forest Gate
London E7 8LE*

Tel: 020-8472-8887

Tube: Upton Park, Forest Gate BR

Tue-Sun: 2.00-22.30,

closed Mon

Wild Cherry

Recently refurbished vegetarian restaurant, which has a light, spacious feel to it, combined with elegant décor. Sit inside and enjoy the ambience or pop outside to the secluded garden and take a break from the city.

Vegan soup of the day and a huge range of salads.

For mains there is always a vegan option or two, like aubergine and courgette pilau plus salad £4.50; or veg with spicy & fruity peanut sauce and rice £4.25.

Wide range of homebaked cakes, including vegan, sugar-free and wheat-free, such as banoffee pie £2.25, carrot cake or chocolate brownies.

Next to the London Buddhist Centre and many meditators pop in before or after classes to enjoy a vast range of herbal teas, home made lemonade and cordials, iced coffee or ginger iced tea-punch, tea, fresh coffee, organic GM-free soya milk and soya milkshakes. No booze so bring your own and pay £1 corkage.

Jambala bookshop next door and Evolution gift shop opposite, all linked to the Buddhist centre next door. Outside catering and cakes. 3 highchairs. Wheelchair access. Discounts for HIV+. They also exhibit art. Formerly called The Cherry Orchard.

241 Globe Road
Bethnal Green
London E2 0JD

Tel: 020-8980 6678

Tube: Bethnal Green

Mon: 11.00–15.00.
Tue–Fri:
11.00–19.00.

Closed Sat–Sun.

EAST END Vegetarian restaurants

Thai Garden

Thai vegetarian and seafood restaurant where you'll pay a lot less than in the West End. Over 40 vegetarian dishes of which many are vegan. Intimate dining on two floors, the staff are friendly and attentive.

Starters £3.50, or £8.00 for a combination platter for 2 people sharing, such as satay shitake mushrooms in peanut sauce, spring rolls, deep fried vegetable tempura. 4 veggie soups £3.50.

There are 14 vegetable main dishes and another 11 noodle and rice dishes, £1.50 to £4.50. Gang phed ped yang jay was full of flavour, consisting of Thai aubergine, mock duck, pineapple, tomatoes, grapes, bamboo shoots and sweet basil leaves in a red curry with coconut cream. Lard na with fried rice noodles, mushrooms, mixed veg and black bean sauce was also very filling. Other dishes include spicy potato deep fried in chilli sauce, or stir-fried morning glory with garlic and chilli for £5.00. And of course there are Pad Thai fried noodles with peanuts, parsnip, bean sprouts and veg.

Desserts include banana with coconut milk £2.50.

House wine £2.00 glass or £7.50 a bottle, beer £1.50. Tea or coffee about £1.50 but no soya milk.

249 Globe Road
Bethnal Green
London E2 0JD

Tel: 020–8981 5748

Tube: Bethnal Green

Mon–Fri:
12.00–15.00 then
18.00–23.00,

Sat–Sun:
18.00–23.00,

EAST END

Vegetarian restaurants

Applejacks

Excellent general healthfood shop. If they don't have it they'll get it within a week. Most of their take-away range is vegan including the Mexican and blackeye bean wraps, pakoras, rolls, tofu pasties, organic soya cheese pasties, bhajis, nut and mushroom pasties. Carrot cake for afters. Small selection of books.

Health food store
& take-away

Unit 28, The Mall
The Stratford Centre
London E15

Tel: 020-8519 5809

Tube: Stratford

Mon-Sat: 9.00-18.00,
Thu/Fri: 9.00-19.00,
Sun: 11.00-16.00

Back To Eden

Completely veggie store with an Afro-Caribbean flavour. They sell organic herbs, food and spices and prepared food and veg. Also veggie and vegan patties, some toiletries and a small range of books. Formerly called Vitality Health Centre.

Health food store
and take-away

120a
Lower Clapton Road
Clapton
London E5 0QR

Tel: 020-8510-9777

Mon- Sat: 10-22.00,
Sun closed

Food & Fitness

Regular health food store specialising in vitamins, supplements and body building. No take-away food.

Health food store

43 Old Church Road
South Chingford
London E4 6JS

Tel: 020-8524 0722

Mon-Sat: 9.00-17.30

Friends Organic

Buddhist wholefood co-op with take-away food and sandwiches, vegan pies and kebabs, which they'll heat up for you. Organic fruit and veg, Fairtrade range and skin-care products . Formerly called Friends Foods.

Wholefoods
& organic shop

83 Roman Road
London E2 0GQ

Tel: 0181-980 1843

Mon- Sat:
9.30-18.00,

Tues: 10.00-18.00,

Fri: 9.30-19.00

Ghir Health Foods & Chemist

Selection of dry wholefoods, body building supplements, cruelty-free cosmetics, nickel free jewellery, Bach flower remedies and snacks.

Health foods
store

426-428 Barking
Road
London E6 3BD

Tel: 020-8471 7576

Mon-Fri:
9.00-19.00,

Sun closed,

on chemist rota so it
may be open late.

Granary Health Foods

Usual range includes some organic food, vitamins and minerals, vegan ice-cream and yoghurts.

Health food shop

165 High Street
Eastham
London E6

Tel: 020-8552-5988

Mon–Sat:
9.00–18.30,
Sun closed.

Heroes of Nature

Organic food shop with some fresh veggie take-aways like soups, sandwiches, quiches and cakes, though they stock meat unfortunately.   Also two vegan wines. Small selection of household cleaning products and a few other non-food items.

Organic food shop

20–22 Broadway Market
off Mare Street
Hackney
London E8 4QJ

Tel: 020-7249-1177

Mon–Fri:
9.00–19.00,

Sat: 9.00–19.00,

Sun: 10.00–18.00

Holland & Barrett

Health food shop

Health food store with soya sausage rolls, pasties, but no sandwiches.

90 East Mall
Stratford Centre
London E15 1XQ

Tel: 020-8536 0467

Tube: Stratford

Mon–Sat: 9.00–17.30,
Sun: 10.00–16.00

Holland & Barrett

Health food shop

Health food store with frozen pasties, soya sausage rolls, porkless pies.

Dalston Cross
Shopping Centre
London E8

Tel: 020-7923 9113

Mon–Sat: 9.00–17.30,
Sun: 10.00–16.00

Holland & Barrett

Health food shop

Situated under an office block, this store caters for the surrounding workers. Small take-away selection along with dried foods, supplements and toiletries.

Aldgate Barrs Centre
1 Whitechapel High St
London E1 1AA

Tel: 020-7481-3791

Tube: Aldgate east

Mon–Fri: 08.00–17.00,
Sat–Sun closed

Honey Health Foods

This shop concentrates on having a wide range of health supplements, vitamins and minerals, many of which are suitable for veggies and vegans. They also have some organic herbal teas, cereals, rice cakes, dried fruit, nuts, seeds, pulses and the Ecover range of cleaning products. Formerly called Nutters of Woodford.

Health food shop

83 High Road
Woodford
London E18 2QP

Tel: 020-85306136

Mon Sat:
9.30–17.30,

Sun closed

Nature's Choice

Health food shop with organic bread, magazines and books, cosmetics and a small savoury and sweet take-away selection. Formerly called Vanns Health Store.

Health food shop

47 Church Lane
Leytonstone
London E11 1HE

Tel:
020-8539-4196

Mon–Sat:
9.00–18.30,
Sun closed

Peaches

Large range for a small shop. Apart from the usuals they stock organic English fruit wines and vegan wines. A good range of take-away food and veggie snacks available some days.

143 High Street
Wanstead
London E11 2RL

Tel: 020–8530 3617

Tues–Sat:
9.00–18.00,
Sun & Mon closed

Second Nature Wholefoods

Good selection of organic foods, supplements and sandwiches, pasties and pies and various snacks for veggie and vegans. The focus is on fresh and packaged organic produce and they cater for special diets. They also stock a veggie and cruelty-free range of toiletries, handmade cards, fair-traded gifts, incense, oil burners etc.
Local deliveries

Wholefoods
& take–away

78 Wood Street
Walthamstow
London E17 3HX

Tel: 020–8520 7995

Mon–Sat:
8.00–17.30,
Sun closed

EAST END

Wholefood & health food shops

218

The Wholemeal Shop

Vegetarian shop with good range that includes organic bread, vitamins, body-building products, range of veggie take-away options and vegan ice-cream.

Health food shop

190 Wells Street
London E9 6QT

Tel: 020-8985-1822

Mon– Sat: 9.00–18.00,
Sun closed

Veenus Health Food

Specialise in teas and vitamins, dry whole-foods. Not exclusively veggie but stock many veggie and vegan foods and organic ranges.
And yes, the name is spelt correctly.

Health food shop

141C High Street
Walthamstow
London E17 7DB

Tel: 020-8520-3085

Mon–Sat: 9.00–18.00,
Sun closed

Vita Health

Usual range of wholefoods and chilled and frozen veggie foods including veggie sausages and burgers, but no fresh take-away. Small toiletries section with cruelty-free shampoos and soaps and a few books. Vitamins and supplements including Solgar.

Wholefoods shop

565 Lee Bridge Road
Leyton
London E10 7EQ

Tel: 020-8539- 245

Mon–Sat: 9.00–18.00
Sun closed

Wholefood & health food shops

A delightful way ...

Spitalfields Organic Market

Open Sundays from 9am–2pm and only 5 minutes walk from Liverpool Street Station. The market is a covered area with lots of craft stalls and good quality second-hand goods.

Excellent organic fresh fruit and veg as well as dried, tinned and other processed organic foods.

There is an east Asian style food market with a wide range of foods where you can eat café style or take-away, and a falafel café. A great place to meet your friends.

Organic fruit & veg Market

Commercial Street London E1

Tube: Liverpool St.

Sunday 9am–2pm

... to spend Sunday morning.

EAST END Wholefood & health food shops

Spitalfields Organics

Completely vegetarian wholefood shop with a selection of take-away pies and pasties, plenty of which are vegan. Also a range of organic and non-organic products including toiletries.

103a Commercial Street
Spitalfields
London E1

Tel:
020-7377 8909

Tube:
Liverpool Street

Mon–Fri:
9.30–19.00,

Sat: 10.00–19.00,

Sun: 9.00–19.00

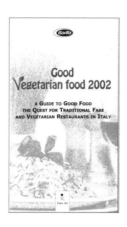

VEGETARIAN ITALY

by the Italian Vegetarian Association

Arranged by region, this beautiful book offers a detailed list of restaurants and accommodation, with addresses, prices and opening times, plus descriptions of the areas, cultural and historical attractions, regional food specialities and recipes (vegetarian and vegan), local festivals, products and wines.

There are photos of the Italian vegetarian recipes, reason enough to buy the book even if you don't go to Italy this year. 128 pages, full colour throughout.

£6.99 + postage mail order only from Vegetarian Guides
See order form at the end of this guide or
www.vegetarianguides.co.uk

West London

Places in West London

Vegetarian restaurants

Omnivorous restaurants

Wholefood shops

Blah Blah Blah

Vegetarian
restaurant & take-away

78 Goldhawk Road
Shepherds Bush
London W12 8HA

Tel: 020 8746 1337

Tube:
Shepherds Bush

Mon-Sat:
12.30-14.30
& 19.00-23.00,
Sun: 19.00-23.00
(varies, phone first)

Vegetarian restaurant on two floors near Shepherds Bush Green. International menu. One starter and one main dish are always vegan and they can sometimes veganize certain dishes.

Six hot or cold appetisers like rolled aubergine kofta £4.95, mushroom galette with white wine sauce £5.95.

Five main courses £9.50 such as Thai green curry with basmati rice and fruit salsa; vegetable pie and chips with onion gravy .

Desserts £4.95, but not a single vegan one, they say there is no demand. No demand for Tofutti ice-cream?

No booze so bring your own and pay £1.25 corkage per person. No credit cards.

Vegan Thai Buffet

Vegan
buffet restaurant

167 The Vale
Acton
London W3

Tel: 020-8740 0888

Tube:
Shepherds Bush

Every day
12.00-22.00,
Sun 17.30-22.00

New oriental vegan buffet restaurant west of Shepherds Bush where you can eat as much as you like for just £5, £3 take-away.

Eat till you explode from boiled and stir-fried rice, spring rolls, tofu, stir-fry veg, soya meats and noodles.

WEST LONDON Vegetarian restaurants

The Gate Vegetarian Restaurant

Top class international vegetarian restaurant. Unique setting in an artist's studio with modernist leanings.

9 starters (7 vegan options) £1.95–£8.50 like potato cake with veg & herbs; parsnip & caramelised red onion risotto; Greek filo pastry of lentils, butterbean and spinach.

6 mains, 4 vegan, such as pan-fried mushrooms with polenta, plus cannelini bean and artichoke salsa, finished with truffle oil glazed spinach leaves at £10.50; Malaysian curry with basmati and wild rice, garnished with papaya salsa £9.50.

6 desserts, 3 vegan, like damson and pear crumble with vegan ice-cream or sorbet. House wine £9.75 bottle, £2.95 glass. Veggie wines and beers, coffees and herb teas, and they have soya milk. Credit cards accepted. Smoking allowed in restaurant. Book at least 2 days ahead at the weekend.

51 Queen Caroline St
Hammersmith
London W6 9QL

Tel: 020–8748 6932

Tube: Hammersmith

Lunch –Mon–Sat:
12.00–15.00,
dinner: 18–23.00,

Sun closed

Vegetarian restaurants   WEST LONDON

Indigo

New Indo-Chinese vegetarian restaurant, set in a complex with a cinema and bowling alley and a friendly lively atmosphere.

The menu has South Indian and several Indo-Chinese offerings with dosas and noodles, £3–6.50.

Lunchtime buffet £4.99 12.00–14.30 during the week.

*Unit 1, Royale
Leisure Park,
Kendal Avenue (off
Western Avenue
(A40),
London W3 OPA*

Tel: 020–8992 1212

Tube: Park Royal

Every day 12–23.00

Sagar

Indian vegetarian
restaurant

New South Indian vegetarian restaurant that opened December 2002, near the Town Hall.

Three courses for around £10–11.

Some vegan food as they use both vegetable or butter ghee in different dishes.

Licensed. Smoking area. Visa, MC, Amex.

*157 King St,
Hammersmith,
London W6*

Tel: 020–8741 8563

*Tube:
Hammersmith*

*Mon–Fri 12–15.00,
17.30–22.30;*

Sat–Sun 12–22.30

WEST LONDON Vegetarian restaurants

Garden Café

Friendly omnivorous café, stylishly decorated, which always has some veggie meals, sometimes vegan. The London Lighthouse is a hostel and home to people suffering from AIDS and offers discount on meals to HIV sufferers. On summer days the French windows open out onto a peaceful and relaxing garden.

Good quality food at very reasonable prices with meals around £4.00, such as pasta, stuffed peppers or aubergine with rice or bulgur, served with veg. Salad bar with some vegan items at 60p per portion. Baked potatoes.

Coffee, tea, juice. Licensed by prior arrangement with the management. Cannot accept credit cards.

*The London Lighthouse
111–117 Lancaster Road.
London W11*

Tel: 020–7792 1200

Tube: Ladbroke Grove

*Mon–Thurs:
9.00–21.00,
Fri: 9.00–18.00,
Sat: 11.00–17.00,*

Sun closed

The Grain Shop

Vegetarian deli, take–away and bakery that uses organic flour. 5 hot dishes, half of which are suitable for vegans, like tofu stir–fry, veg curry or ratatouille, as well as salads all made on the premises

Specialist breads and cakes for allergy free diets, also gluten–free pastries and sugar–free items.

*269a Portobello Road
Notting Hill
London W11*

Tel: 020–7229–5571

*Mon–Sat:
9.30–18.00,*

Sun closed

Byblos Mezza of Lebanon

Lebanese
omnivorous

262 Kensington High
Kensington
London W8 6ND

Tel: 020–7603 4422

Tube:
High St. Kensington

Open every day
11.45–23.45

Lebanese vegetarian and vegan set meal at this omnivorous restaurant with about 10 different hot and cold mezze which consist of pulses, hummous, falafel, tabouleh, vegetables, pastries, rice, dolma etc plus dessert for around £11.85. Individual mezze dishes for £3.65. Lebanese beer £3.45 bottle. House wine £10.85 bottle, glass £3.45. Pot of mint tea £1.85, Turkish coffee £1.85. 10% discount for Vegetarian or Vegan Society, Viva!, PETA with card or advertisement. Also take–away.

Kalamaras Restaurant

Greek
omnivorous

66 Inverness Mews
Bayswater
London W2 3JQ

Tel: 020–77275082
/9122

Tube:
Bayswater, Queeesway

Every day
17.30–24.00,
last order 23.00

Mediterranean Greek omnivorous taverna in a veggieless area on the north side of Hyde Park, close to Paddington Station. Vegetarians can try lots of starters for £2.50-3.50 such as aubergine dip or fresh artichoke hearts casseroled with broad beans and dill. In fact veggies and vegans can concoct a good meal of starters, or try the new vegetarian moussaka £8.00, made with layers of sauteed potatoes, aubergines, courgettes and mushrooms topped with bechamel sauce which can be omitted for vegans for a bit less money.
Bring your own wine and there's no corkage. There's an Oddbins off–license nearby in Queensway with Greek wines or Cullens is even closer. Tea £1, coffee £1.50.

WEST LONDON

Omnivorous restaurants

Wagamama Kensington

Omnivorous fast food Japanese noodle bar with over nine veggie and vegan dishes. See Bloomsbury, WC1 branch for menu.

260 Kensington High Street
London W8 4PW

Tel: 020-7376 1717
Tube:
High St. Kensington

Mon–Sat 11–23.00,
Sun 12.30–22.30

As Nature Intended

Organic &
healthfood shop

Completely organic store that aims to combine the variety of a supermarket with the product range found in traditional health food shops. Many items are suitable for those with food allergies such as sugar-, gluten-, salt- or yeast-free.

201 Chiswick High Road
Chiswick
London W4

Tel: 020-8742-8838

Mon–Fri:
9.00–20.00,

Wide range including sandwiches and pies to take away. Daily deliveries of bread and gluten-free muffins.

Sat 9.00–19.00,

Many tofu-based foods, herbal and homeopathic remedies, aromatherapy oils, beauty and skincare products.

Sun 11.00–17.30

Vegan and veggie wines are clearly labelled and there is a leaflet in case you're unsure what constitutes a vegan wine.

There are two trained nutritionists in-house most afternoons for dietary advice.

WEST LONDON

Health food & wholefood shops

Bushwacker Wholefoods

Vegetarian wholefood shop that is completely GMO free. Plenty for vegans, as well as organic fruit and veg. Speciality product ranges include macrobiotic and gluten-free. Household, skin and body-care, books and aromatherapy oils. There is a noticeboard inside the shop and they use the window to inform customers on campaign issues which affect food, especially GMO.

132 King Street
Hammersmith
London W6 OQU

Tel: 020-8748-2061

Mon–Sat 9.30–18.00,
Tues: 10.00–18.00,
Thurs 9.30–19.00,

Sun closed

Coltsfoot and Kelp

Wholefood shop

This wholefood shop sells the usual produce. No fresh take-away section but a well stocked freezer. They also have household products and homeopathic ranges.

106 Northfields
Avenue
London W13 9RT

Tel: 020-8567-3548

Mon–Sat:
9.30–17.30,

Sun closed

WEST LONDON Health food & wholefood shops

Fresh & Wild

Huge wholefood and organic supermarket on three floors with a staggering array of foods from all over the world, lots of fruit and veg, wines and beers, take-away snacks, remedies, body care and books.

Wholefoods & organic store

210 Westbourne Grove
Notting Hill
London W11 2RH

Tel:
020-7229-1063

Tube: Notting Hill Gate (7 min)

Open:
Mon –Sat :
8.00-20.00, Sun 10-18.00

Health, My God Given Wealth

Organic ranges of bread and various health foods, cruelty-free cosmetics and toiletries.

Good selection of vegan take-away food and snacks such as falafels, rotis, burgers, and sandwiches. The only shop we know in London that stocks a wide range of fresh organic baby food made in Chiswick. Display board for alternative practitioners and local info.

Organic healthfoods shop

41 Turnham Green Terrace
London W4 1RG

Tel: 020-8995-4906

Tube:
Turnham Green

Mon–Fri:
9.30-18.30,
Sat: 9.00-18.00,

Sun closed

Holland & Barrett

Small health food store with no fridge so no take-aways.

Healthfoods shop

260 High Street
Kensington
London W8 6NA

Tel: 020-7603 2751

Tube:
High St. Kensington

Mon-Sat: 9.00-17.30,
closed Sun

Holland & Barrett

Health food shop with some take-aways like pasties.

Healthfoods shop

32 Queensway
Bayswater
London W2 4QW

Tel: 020-7727 6449

Tube: Queensway

Mon-Fri : 9.00-20.00,
Sat: 10.00-20.00
Sun: 11.00-20.00

Holland & Barrett

Small health food store with no fridge so no take-aways.

Healthfoods shop

139 Church St
Kensington
London W8 7EN

Tel: 020-7727 9011

Mon-Sat 9-17.30

Holland & Barrett

Small take-away section and some frozen food available at this store.

416 Chiswick High Rd
Chiswick
London W4 5TF

Tel: 020-8994-1683

Mon-Sat : 9.00-17.30,
Sun: 11.00-16.00

Holland & Barrett

Health food store with a few take-aways like soya sausage rolls.

Health food shop

Unit 13, Kings Mall
King St
Hammersmith
London W6 0DP

Tel 020-8748 9792

Mon-Sat 9-17.30,
Sun 11-16.30

Holland & Barrett

Health food store opposite the Central Line tube station with some savouries take-away food like soya sausage rolls.

Health food shop

112 Shepherds Bush
Centre
Shepherds Bush
London W12 5PP

Tel: 020-8743 1045

Tube: Shepherds Bush

Mon-Sat: 9.30-18.00

Market Place Health Foods

Vegetarian health food shop, with cosmetics and aromatherapy supplies. Impressive range of take-away foods such as veggie samosas, vegetable couscous, chickpea salad, rotis, spring rolls and various salads at around £1.60 each. And they have vegan ice-cream!

8 Market Place
Acton
London W3

Tel: 020-8993-3848

Tube: Acton

Mon–Sat:
9.00–17.45,

Sun closed

Millenium Healthfoods

Health food shop

Health food shop with supplements and wholefoods. No fresh take away, but has a freezer counter. Also household goods, Ecover, body care products, homeopathic remedies and aromatherapy oils. Formerly called Victoria Health Foods

Unit 50b Ealing
Broadway Centre
Ealing
London W5

Tel: 020-8840-6949

Mon–Sat:
9.00–18.00,
Sun: 11.00–17.00

WEST LONDON Health food & wholefood shops

Planet Organic

Organic supermarket

Picnic heaven. Load up here with every kind of veggie food and heaps you never even knew existed. 15 aisles makes this one of the largest retailers of gorgeous organic foods and alcoholic and non-alcoholic drinks, environmentally friendly household goods and exotic flowers in the UK.

Not all vegetarian but the non-veggie stuff is right at the back out of sight. No artificial additives in anything, no hydrogenated fat and no refined sugar. Juice and coffee bar. Great book section includes Veggie Guides.

42 Westbourne Grove
Westbourne Grove
London W2 5SH

Tel: 020-7221 7171

Tube: Bayswater

Mon–Sat:
9.30–20.00,
Sun 12–18.00

Portobello Whole Foods

Healthfoods & wholefoods shop

Excellent large health and wholefood shop in Portobello market area.

Fresh take-aways most days like sandwiches and snacks, some vegan.

Organic fruit and veg.

Vitamins and supplements. Three types of biodegradable cleaning product, and small range of toiletries including soaps, toothpastes and moisturisers.

Unit 1,
266 Portobello Road
Ladbroke Grove
London W10 5TY

Tel: 020-8968 9133

Mon–Sat:
9.30–18.00,
Sun: 11:00–17.00

VEGETARIAN SPAIN
by Jean-Claude Juston.

over 100 vegetarian and vegan restaurants throughout Spain. Includes Alicante, Barcelona, Gerona, Granada, Las Palmas, Madrid, Malaga, Mallorca, Seville, Tenerife. More than just a dining guide with things to do in each area, places to see and shop, and even some Spanish vegan recipes for when you get home. 130 pages.

£7.99 + postage, mail order only from Vegetarian Guides
See order form at the end of this guide or
www.vegetarianguides.com

South London

Places in Waterloo & the South Bank

Vegetarian restaurants

Omnivorous restaurants

Coffee and bars

Wholefood & health food shops

SOUTH LONDON

Vegetarian restaurants

Coopers

Long established (20 years now) vegetarian family run deli with café close to Waterloo. All café dishes are cooked fresh on the day on the premises. The café seats around 17 people.

They serve a variety of vegan savouries like potato and onion bhaji, veg and sunflower rissole, carrot and onion cutlet, chickpea roti, various kebabs and cottage pies. Several types of sandwich like veg sausage and pickle, Swiss herb paté and houmous, peanut butter, all with salad. Appetizers too, for example olives, vine leaves and houmous. They always have a selection of salads with a minimum of one vegan. Soup is often vegan too.

Normally a choice of 5 cakes daily like chocolate and walnut, carrot and coconut, apple and sultana, at least one is vegan.

Also organic beers and ciders, vegan take-away items, and health food shop produce.

17 Lower Marsh
Waterloo
London SE1

Tel: 020-7261-9314

Tube: Waterloo

Mon-Fri:
08.30-17.30

SOUTH LONDON Vegetarian restaurants

Meson Don Felipe

Omnivorous Spanish bar with 10 vegetarian tapas snacks like lentils and fresh vegetables, artichoke heart salad, chickpeas with spinach, and deep fried aubergines for £3.50–4.50.

House wine from £10 to £70 a bottle.

It gets crowded prior to performances at either the Old or Young Vic theatres nearby.

53A The Cut
Waterloo
London SE1 8LF

Tel:
020–7928– 3237

Tube: Waterloo

Mon–Sat:
12.00–24.00,

closed Sun

Tas Restaurant

Turkish omnivorous. Anatolian restaurant that received the *Time Out* Best Vegetarian Meal Award 2000. Almost all starters (meze) are veggie. The menu has a veggie section with 10 main dishes.

Cold starters £2.95 to £3.45 include kisir: crushed walnuts, hazelnuts, bulgar wheat, tomato sauce, herbs, fresh mint, and spring onions; zetinyagli patlican: aubergine, tomatoes, garlic, peppers and chickpeas cooked in olive oil; and the classic Turkish dolma: stuffed vine leaves with pine kernels. Also several veggie hot starters £2.15–£3.45 like sebzeli kofte, which is falafel with broad beans.

Vegetarian main dishes £5.75–6.75 such as patlicamli: grilled aubergine with tomatoes, peppers and couscous; spinach with potaotes; okra with herbs; or biber dolmasi: green pepper, bulgar, parsley, mint, dill and onions. Four veggie salads and the usual rice dishes like bademli pilaf with almonds and kayisili pilaf with apricot for £1.45 to £2.95.

Typical Turkish sweet baklava for dessert, tiny filo pastry parcels stuffed with walnuts and pistachios in syrup. Vegans need to ask which ones are without honey.

Tas is fully licensed and accepts most credit cards. Their menu promises to cater for any special dietary requirements.

Turkish Anatolian restaurant

33 The Cut
Waterloo
London SE1 8LF

Tel: 020–7928–1444

Tube: Waterloo

Mon–Sat:
12 noon –23.30,

Sun 12–22.30

SOUTH LONDON Omnivorous restaurants

One World Shop

Fair trade shop that has limited opening hours as it is staffed by volunteers. (They are always after more helpers.)

Some veggie foods, tea, coffee, chocolate. Also stationery, crafts and clothing.

St John's Church
73 Waterloo Road
Waterloo
London SE1 8TY

Tel: 020-7401-8909

Tube: Waterloo

Open:
limited to Thurs
11.00–16.00,
Fri 11.30–15.00,
Sat 10–12.00

Wholefood & health food shops   SOUTH LONDON

Places in Brixton & Clapham

Vegetarian restaurants

Omnivorous restaurants

Wholefood & health food shops

Cafe Pushkar

Vegetarian cafe and restaurant near Brixton market, now moved to new premises and open in the evenings.

Soup, falafel, veg sausages and burgers start at £2.50. Variety of salads, small £2.50 or large £3.40.

Substantial mains £4–5 like sesame tofu with pineapple and mange-tout, or Thai green curry.

Crumbles, cakes and fruit salads for £1.00 and upwards. All cakes cooked on the premises are vegan.

Soya milkshakes, soya cappuccinos. Fresh organic juices £2.50.

Wine from £8.50 bottle, £2.50 glass.

Lots of papers to read. Children's portions. High chairs.

424 Coldharbour Lane
Brixton
London SW9

Tel: 020–7738–6161

Tube: Brixton

Open:
every day
11.00–23.00

Directions:
Turn left out of Brixton tube, walk past the bus stops and turn left at KFC. It's just past a noodle bar.

SOUTH LONDON Vegetarian restaurants

Cicero's

Vegetarian park café on Clapham Common, near the tube station, in what looks like a converted prefab. International menu and outside seating with some cover for up to 100. Under new ownership but they've kept the old formula and it remains a great place to meet your friends and chill out. 50% vegan. Daily changing menu from 12pm.

All day full veggie breakfast £5 with huge coffee or tea, £5.50 with (soya) capuccino. Starters £3.50 like sushi with dipping sauce, Taj Mahal soup with bread, Moroccan stuffed aubergine with red pepper sauce.

Main courses £5.50 such as char grilled tofu with peanut sauce and Singapore rice; aubergine moussaka; pumpkin and chickpea pie curry with rice. Small salad £2, large £3, largest £4.50.

Sandwiches, can be made with ciabatta, £1.75-3.50. Veggieburger special £5.00 with salad. Also beans or mushrooms on toast from £2.50.

Desserts £2-2.50 include vegan chocolate cake, vegan cherry crunch, vegan apple crumble.

Selection of organic teas, organic lemonade, cola, ginger ginseng, Aqua Libra, Amé, elderflower, juices. Organic £1-1.25, others 60-80p.

12.5% service change includes corkage if you bring your own booze. No smoking. Cheques but no credit cards. Toys for kids. Only open in the evening for private bookings of 20 to 25 at £20 per head.

2 Rookery Road
Clapham Common
Clapham
London SW4 9DD

Tel: 020-7498 0770

Tube:
Clapham Common

Open daily
10.00-18.00
summer,
10.00_16.00
winter

SOUTH LONDON

Vegetarian restaurants

Sayur Mayur

New Oriental vegetarian restaurant and take-away.

Lots of fake meat and tofu dishes. No MSG.

*Oriental
vegetarian*

*87 Battersea Rise
London SW11*

Tel: 020–7350 0900

*Train:
Clapham Junction BR*

*Every day
17.30–23.00;*

*also Fri–Sun
13.00–15.00*

Eco

The best pizzas are vegetarian according to the manager, though they weren't sure if the dough base was dairy free, however the vegan calzone is great with pepper and aubergine. This is a pizza place with panache, smartly decorated in light wood and sculptured steel.

Allow £7 for a pizza, £10 for a bottle of wine or £3 a glass. The garlic bread is done in olive oil not butter.

Gets pretty crowded so reservations advisable and you are encouraged to leave after an hour and a half, but great fun if you've got the energy.

*Omnivorous
Pizza place*

*162 Clapham High
Street
Clapham
London SW4*

Tel: 020–7978 1108

*Tube:
Clapham Common*

*Daily lunch
12.00–16.00,
then 18.30–22.30,*

*weekends open a bit
longer*

SOUTH LONDON Omnivorous restaurants

Bah Humbug

Vegetarian &
seafood restaurant

Plush vegetarian and seafood restaurant in an atmospheric church crypt with cande-labras, antique furniture and mirrors. Drink the night away in the adjacent Bug Bar till 3am with live music, DJ's, singers and poets evenings – see Time Out for details. Two thirds of the menu is fish and seafood but there's plenty for veggies and precious little else in the area at night.

Four of the six starters £4–£5 are vegetarian or vegan like satay tofu.
4 mains out of 8 are vegetarian, one vegan, but all can be made vegan. Open ravioli comes with artichoke and wild mushrooms, dressed with white truffle oil £9.50. Miso and shitake mushroom risotto £7.50. Wellington en croute of cashews, brazil nuts and almonds £9.20. Mock duck made from soya and wheat £9.50.

Lots of desserts, but no vegan ones. They were curious as to why they don't get many vegans. Well, if you're vegan, you can tell them that vegans don't just eat mains!

Coffee £1.80 to £2.90 with liqueurs, or have a (soya) capuccino, see, they do love vegans really so please encourage them! House wine £9.90 bottle up to £22, £2.80 glass.

Smoking thoughout. Disabled access. Visa, MC. Reservations recommended. Time Out Vegetarian Restaurant Winner 1997.

The Crypt, St. Mathew's Church Brixton Hill (south end) Brixton London SW2

Tel: 020-7738-3184

Tube: Brixton

Mon–Fri: 17.00–22.30,

Fri–Sat: 17.00–23.30

SOUTH LONDON

Omnivorous restaurants

Tea Room des Artistes

Veggie/fish
and wine bar

One third vegetarian, two-thirds sea food and fish restaurant and wine bar in a 16th century barn. Menu changes regularly so phone ahead to see if it suits as there might be a couple of nice veggie dishes on.

Soup of the day served with French or Irish soda bread £3.95, vegan Mediterranean mezze £4.50.

Main course £9.95 could be herbed vegan sausage with mashed potato and thick onion gravy; vegetable korma with dhal, basmati rice, onion bhaji, mango chutney and nan bread.

Sides dishes are all vegan £1.00 to £2.50 like olives and piquillo pepppers, mixed leaf salad.

Desserts £3.75, such as dairy-free ice-cream with summer fruits and raspberry coulis.

2 set courses are £13.50 or 3 set courses for £17.00.

Extensive drinks menu. House wine £10.50 bottle, £2.25 glass.

*697 Wandsworth
Road
Battersea
London SW8 3JF*

Tel: 020-7652 6526

*Tube:
Clapham Common*

*Tue-Sun:
17.30-01.00.*

*Sun:
15.00-12.30am,*

Closed Mon.

SOUTH LONDON Omnivorous restaurants

Jacaranda Garden Restaurant

Omnivorous café with 80% vegetarian food offering great value, next to Brixton market and tube station. Very international with an African and West Indian flavour. Quite a large vegan clientele as many dishes are or can be made vegan.

Main courses include vegetarian gumbo, an okra dish £5.20, west African jollof rice served with salads, or Jamaican rice and peas with salad £3.95. Two substantial vegetarian curries with rice £3.95 or pitta £3.50.

Soups are always veggie £1.95. Pasta with salad £3.95. Italian focaccia bread is very popular here with hot fillings for £3.80. Also Jamaican patties with salad. Vegetarian double decker club sandwich £3.20, can be made vegan with avocado. Desserts include home made cakes £1.40 and pies like pecan £2.25.

Fruit juices or filter coffee £1.10, teas and herbal teas,80p–£1, bottled beers £1.95, wine £2.20 glass.

Smoking on the ground floor, non-smoking upstairs. Cheques but no cards. Disabled access.

Jacaranda Garden Restaurant

11–13 Brixton Station Road Brixton London SW9 8PA

Tel: 020–7274 8383

Tube: Brixton

Mon–Fri: 12.00–17.00,

Sat: 11.00–18.00, closed Sun

SOUTH LONDON

Omnivorous restaurants

Fresh & Wild

Organic wholefood supermarket with a huge range of organic produce, fruit and veg, take-away food, remedies and books.

Café and juice bar with cosy sofas and tables. Also a dedicated deli section up another level via a few steps.

For more info on product lines see the Stoke Newington branch. (page 140)

Organic wholefood supermarket

305-311 Lavender Hill
London SW11 1LN

Tel: 020-7585 1488

Mon-Fri:
9.00-21.00,

Sat: 8.30-19.30,

Sun: 12.00-18.00

Brixton Wholefoods

Large selection of health and wholefoods, huge range of 'serve yourself' herbs and spices which you weigh so you can have as little or as much as you want. Large range of vegan foods including non-dairy cheese and ice-cream. Organic fruit and veg and good take-away selection. Homeopathic remedies.

Health food & wholefoods shop

59 Atlantic Road
Brixton
London SW9

Tel: 020-7737 2210

Tube: Brixton

Mon-Sat:
9.30-17.30,

Fri: 9.00-18.00,

Sun closed

Dandelion Natural Foods

Vegan take–away sweet and savoury food a speciality here. Cooked on the premises with at least 20 options including rice dishes, lasagne, spring rolls, bhajis, samosas, salads, burgers, cutlets, cakes (sometimes vegan) etc. Organic fruit and veg arrives Tuesday and Thursday. Many other oganic products.

120 Northcote Road
Battersea
London SW11 6QU

Tel:: 020–7350 0902

Mon–Sat:
9.00–18.00,

Sun:
12.00–15.00

Holland & Barrett

Health food shop

Plenty of veggie and vegan food stuffs to be had at this branch of the popular high-street health food shops found all over the U.K.

Unit 29, The Arndale
Wandsworth
London SW18 4DG

Tel: 020–8871 3706

Mon–Fri:
9.00–17.30,

Sat 9.00–17.00,

Sun closed

SOUTH LONDON

Wholefood & health food shops

Holland & Barrett

This branch has a freezer section and small amount of take-away food.

51 St Johns Rd
Clapham
London SW11 1QP

Tel: 020-7228 6071

Mon–Sat: 9.00–18.00,
Sun: 11.00–16.00

S. G. Manning Pharmacy

Health food shop

Small health food store in a pharmacy towards the south end of Brixton Hill. An astonishing range of wholefoods, non-dairy cheese, organic bread, frozen foods including vegan ice-cream, nut and chocolate spreads. Great for vegans.

34–36 New Park Rd.
Brixton
London SW2

Tel: 020-8647-4391

Mon–Fri: 9.00–18.00,
Sat: 9.15–17.00,

Today's Living

Health food shop

Supplements, oils, frozen foods, remedies and body building products. Sandwiches and pasties, several vegan. They also have freezer counter.

92 Clapham High St.
Clapham
London SW4 7UL

Tel: 020-7622-1772

Mon–Sat: 9.00–18.30

SOUTH LONDON Wholefood & health food shops

Places further South

Vegetarian restaurants

Wholefood & healthfood shops

Ambala Sweets

Vegetarian take-away with Indian sweets, samosas, pakoras and curries, but not vegan. They have another branch in Drummond St, NW1, see our Bloomsbury section.

see our Bloomsbury section.

48 Upper Tooting Road, SW17 7PD

Tel: 020-8767 1747

Tube: Tooting Bec, Tooting Broadway

Mon-Sat: 10.00-20.00, Sun: 10.00-18.00

Domali Café

International café

38 Westow Street Crystal Palace London SE19 3AH

Tel:020-8768-0096

Tube: Crystal Palace BR, Gypsy Hill BR

Mon-Tues: 9.30-18.00,

Wed-Sun: 9.30-23.00

New café that has a big global menu, 90% veggie and plenty for vegans.
Veggie breakfast served until 6pm. For lunch they have vegan soup £2.90. Specials include wild mushroom paté with farmhouse bread, olive oil and mixed leaf garnish £3.90; blackeye and red bean chilli casserole with rice £6.50; layered sweet potato bake with salad £6.90.
Toasties £3.50 include veggie sausage with mustard and tomato, or veggie salami with roasted pepper. Vegan sandwiches include houmous, veggie BLT £2.90.

Coffee and juice bar with soya smoothies, double juices £2.20, singles £1.60. Add a shot of St. John's Wort, echinacea, gurarana or milk thistle for 40p. Large drinks list includes house cocktails and wines. Happy hour every evening 6-8pm.

Child portions are available. Local artists' work is exhibited and it's for sale.

SOUTH LONDON Vegetarian restaurants

259

Bonnington Café

Vegetarian wholefood restaurant and garden in a quiet square. Historically a large squatter community thrived here. Nowadays there are as many Mercs as 2CVs. Run on a cooperative basis with a different cook preparing the food each night from their own repertoire, so there is no set menu. The atmostphere is very laid back and it's great value as you can get a three course meal for around £7.

On the day we visited the main courses £4.50 were roast pepper, red onion and rocket pizza with salad; and spinach and blackeye bean tart with roast potatoes and salad. Roasted butternut squash soup with bread £2.50. Chocolate cake £2. There is usually vegan food.

Corkage is free.

Somethimes there is piano music.

11 Vauxhall Grove
Vauxhall
London SW8 1TA

Tel: no telephone

Tube: Vauxhall

Open every day
19.00–23.00

SOUTH LONDON

Vegetarian restaurants

Kuirk-Schwarz-Waad

Qualified Natural Practitioners

East

Traditional Chinese Medicine
Acupuncture
Ampuka
Chinese Herbs
Cupping
Dietary Therapy
Martial Arts
Macrobiotics
Meditation
Moxibustion
Reiki
Shiatsu

West

Vibrational Energy Medicine
Crystal Therapy
Flower Essences
Homeopathy
Iridology
Naturopathy
Nutrition
Stress Management

Telephone/Fax: 020 8555 1611
Mobile:07985 120 101

e-mail: schwarzwaadkuirk@btopenworld.com

Kastoori

There is an east African influence to this vegetarian Indian Gujarati restaurant which doesn't use eggs.

7 starters are vegan such as Mogo bhajia, bhel (mix of puffed rice, sev, potato and onions in a sweet and sour sauce), or dahi vada (crispy puris filled with diced potatoes,chickpeas, pani puri sauce and sweet and sour sauce and topped with sev) £1.95 to £2.75.

12 curries , 8 vegan. You could try the Kastoori kofta – mixed vegetable balls, roasted aubergine curry, or a potato curry with the chef's sauce.

Thalis 8.25 to £15.75.

Other dishes include dosas, and the range of Kastoori family specials like Kasodi – which is sweetcorn in coconut milk with ground peanut sauce, or kontola curry – made with a crunchy mountain vegetable with garlic sauce.

Lots of side dishes, plus a choice of six desserts – alas only one vegan, the fresh fruit.

188 Upper Tooting Road
Tooting
London SW17 7EJ

Tel: 020-8767 7027

Tube:
Tooting Broadway

Mon-Tues:
18.00-22.30
Wed-Sun:
12.30-14.30.
then 18-22.30.

SOUTH LONDON

Vegetarian restaurants

Mantanah Thai Cuisine

Thai restaurant in deepest sarf London near Croydon. Like many Thai restaurants, this one has as many veggie dishes as some vegetarian restaurants.

Starters from £3.50–4.70 like spring roll, golden veg with pepper, sweet potato and plum sauce, deep fried pumpkin, tom yum soup, spicy mushrooms with coconut milk.

Main dishes include the Thai classics of red and green curry £5.25 plus steamed, coconut or sticky rice. You could also try the exotic spicy banana flower with oyster mushrooms and steamed sweet potato. Choice of salads.

Licensed for wine and beer including Thai Singha beer.

2 Orton Buildings
Portland Road
South Norwood
London SE25 4UD

Tel: 020-8771 1148

Tube:
Norwood Junction
(Thameslink)

Tue–Sun:
18.30–23.00.

Closed Mon.

SOUTH LONDON Vegetarian restaurants

Mangoes

Brand new colourful vegetarian and vegan café and take-away in Wimbledon. Moghul influences beautiful wood carvings on the walls. The food is a fusion of modern British and Mediterranean favourites with classic Indian dishes, plus some great vegan cakes.

Lunch includes sandwiches £1.30-£2.40, or create your own by appending items pizza-style for 10p to 60p per item. Sandwiches include aubergine paté, veggie bacon, cashew nut butter. Or have a 5 or 10 round sandwich platter £8.50-£19.00 with lots of different ingredients served on organic wholemeal or white bread.

Baked potato or rice in a bowl topped with dhal, chilli, curry, baked beans, aubergine paté or hummous in small, medium or large sizes 1.70-£2.80. Pasta and soup £1.20-£2.40, 20p less if you're taking away.

Many home-made sweets include (vegan) sundaes for £3.50, and some cakes are vegan from £1.30.

Hot and cold drinks 60p-£1.40. Also smoothies for £1.80 regular, £2.20 large.

Mangoes also do catering.

Veggie / vegan café & take-away

191-193 Hartfield Road
Wimbledon
London SW19 3TH

Tel:
020-8542 9912

Tube:
Wimbledon

Open:
Mon-Fri 7- 17.00,
Sat 9-17.00, Sun 11-16.00

Milan Vegetarian Restaurant

Gujarati and South Indian vegetarian restaurant and sweet centre with over half the dishes being vegan (or vegan option) and clearly marked on the menu.

16 starters (13 are vegan) £1.60–2.50 like mogo chips, bhajias, spring rolls, kachori, puris, patties.

They offer 22 main courses (16 vegan), divided into either dosa or curries for £2.50 to £4.95, like veg kofta, mushroom curry, chana bhatura chick pea and potato curry with fried fluffy bread.

Three thalis, £4.95–£7.95. Milan special thali has a vegan option for £7.95 with millet loaf, roast aubergine, moong, rice and papadum. All the usual parathas, nan, dahl, pickles.

8 desserts £1.25–£2.00, two of which are vegan.

Juices like fresh passion and mango from £2.25. House wine £6.50 bottle, £2.00 glass.

Milan does catering for weddings and parties. All major cards accepted.

158 Upper Tooting Road
Tooting
London SW17 7ER

Tel:
020–8767 4347

Tube:
Tooting Bec, Tooting Broadway

Open:
Mon 11–21.30,
Tues–Thur 10–21.30, Fri –Sat 9.–22.00, Sun 9–21.30

SOUTH LONDON Vegetarian restaurants

Shahee Bhelpoori

Indian vegetarian restaurant with 100 dishes, many of them vegan and virtually anything can be made vegan for you.

Starters £1.85–3.05 like vegetable kebab. Side orders from £2.25 include vegetable kofta at £2.50.

Main courses from £2.95 include several dosas from £4.10. 10 thalis £4.50–6.95.

14 desserts from £1.85 including vegan ice cream and hazelnut crunch.. Hooray, an Indian restaurant that recognises vegans don't just eat main courses, which might help explain their popularity with local vegans. And who says you need to be vegan to eat vegan dessert? Do you have to be Indian to eat curry?

Exotic Sunday and weekday buffet lunches only £3.95, eat as much as you like.

Beer £1.85 pint, wine £6.50 bottle or £1.60 glass. Tea 60p, coffee 90p, soya milk available.

10% discount to Vegetarian or Vegan Society members. Visa, DC. If you present this book you also get 10% discount. On the A23 Brighton to London road. Croydon Vegans meet here, see local contacts.

1547 London Road
Opposite Norbury
British Rail Station
Norbury
London SW16 4AD

Tel: 020–8679 6275

Train:
Norbury BR

Open every day
12.00–14.30,
18–23.00,

Sun Lunch
12.00–15.00

SOUTH LONDON

Vegetarian restaurants

266

Wholemeal Café

Wholefood vegetarian restaurant with Thai, Indian, Mediterranean and world cuisine. Large vegan selection.

Typical dishes include garlic mushrooms with salad and pitta £2.90; guacamole and warm pitta £2.85, or soup of the day £2.20, usually vegan.
Main dishes £2.90–6.25 include homity pie, hot bake of the day, casserole of the day, red Thai curry, spinach and mushroom crumble.

Desserts £2.25 such as banoffee pie or wholemeal fruit crumble with vegan custard–also at £2.25.

Organic wines, beers, ciders, ales, soft drinks like Aaqua Libra and organic lemonade.

Wholefood
vegetarian restaurant

1 Shrubbery Road
Streatham
London SW16 2AS

Tel: 020-8769 2423

Tube: Streatham BR,
Streatham Hill BR

Open every day
12.00–22.00

closed on all bank
holidays

As Nature Intended

Younger sister store to the popular Chiswick branch, completely organic, they aim to combine the variety of a super-market with the product range found in a traditional healthfood shop.

Friendly and well trained staff on hand including a nutritionist and visiting homeopath. Most weekends they have product sampling such as chocolate and (vegan) wine.

For product ranges see the Chiswick, W4 branch. (page 232)

For product ranges see the Chiswick, W4 branch. (page 232)

*Health food &
organic foods shop*

*270–274 Upper
Richmond Road
East Sheen
London SW14 9JE*

Tel: 020–8878–0627

Tube:

*Mon–Fri:
9.00–20.00,*

Sat: 9.00–19.00,

Sun: 11.00–17.30

Baldwins Health Food Shop

Hot and cold take-away selection of sweet and savoury goodies, also supplements and green toiletries. They no longer stock organic fruit and veg. Informative notice-board.

*Healthfoods &
take–away*

*270–274 Upper
Richmond Road
East Sheen
London SW14 9JE*

Tel: 020–8878–0627

*Mon–Fri: 9.00–20.00,
Sat: 9.00–19.00,
Sun: 11.00–17.30*

Balham Wholefood & Health Store

Health food shop with a large range of dried fruit, seeds, pulses etc, both organic and non-organic, and books.

Discount of 5% to Vegetarian and Vegan Society members.

8 Bedford Hill
Balham
London SW12 9RG

Tel:
020-8673-4842

Tube:

Open:
Mon–Sat 9.30–18.00,
Tue & Thu –19.00;
closed for lunch
13.00–14.00

GNC

One of a new chain of health food shops. Dried fruit, seeds, nuts etc. Freezer products like veggie sausages and burgers and veggie mincee. Herbs, vegan chocolate, books, but no fresh take-aways at this branch. Large range of vitamins and minerals, some veggie and vegan.

Formerly called Health & Diet Centre.

151 Putney High Street
Putney
London SW15 1SU

Tel: 020-8788-0944

Mon–Sat
9.00–18.00,

Thurs: 9.00–19.00,

Sun: 11.00–17.00

GNC

Health food shop

Part of national chain of health food shops. No take-away items available here but they have a freezer section. Formerly called Health & Diet Centre.

Centre Court
Shopping Centre
Queens Road
Wimbledon
London SW19

Tel: 020-8947 3583

Mon–Sat:
9.30–19.00,

Thurs: 9.30–20.00,
Sat 9.30–18.00,
Sun 11–17.00

Wholefood & health food shops **SOUTH LONDON**

Greenlands Health

It's a bit of a veggie desert in Greenwich since two of the veggie restaurants there closed, so take advantage of this great little place. Take-aways include pies, pasties, snacks £1.25–£2. Sandwiches start at £1.49, salads £1.69. Also some cakes and health drinks.

Unit 3a, Greenwich Craft Market
Greenwich
London SE10 9HZ

Tel:
020–8293 9176

Tube: Greenwich

Mon–Sun:
9.30–18.30

Greenwich Organics

Organic healthfood shop

Small organic healthfood shop with fruit and veg, breads, some books and gifts and green toiletries.
Formerly called All Things Nice.

86 Royal Hill
Greenwich
London SE10

Tel: 020–8488 6764

Tube: Greenwich

Mon–Fri:
10.00–18.00,

Sat: 10.00–17.30,

Sun closed

SOUTH LONDON Wholefood & health food shops

Health & Diet Centre

Large well stocked shop in picturesque village just off Blackheath Common. Take-away with vegan hot and cold food and good selection of breads. Occasional free tastings on Saturdays! They still offer 10% discount to Vegan and Vegetarian Society members, and to senior citizens on Thursday.

31 Tranquil Vale
Blackheath
London SE3

Tel: 020-8318 0448

Mon–Sat:
9.00–18.00,

Sun closed

Health Food Centre

Health food shop

Health foods like dried fruit, nuts and seeds, but no fresh take-away or cruelty-free cosmetics here. Vitamins, homeopathic remedies, aromatherapy oils.

156 Balham High
Road
Balham
London SW12 9BN

Tel: 020-8265 7532

Mon–Sat:
9.00–18.00,

Sun closed

Wholefood & health food shops | SOUTH LONDON

272

Health Zone Ltd

Health food shop with complementary therapy clinic attached. They stock a wide range of veggie and vegan foods, supplements and body-care products. Also veggie/vegan sandwiches, pastiees, pies from £2 upwards and a gluten -free range. Vegan ice-cream.

30 Wimbledon Hill Road
Wimbledon
London SW19 7PA

Tel: 020-8944-1133

Mon–Fri:
11.00–19.00,

Sat: 9.30–18.00,

Sun 11–17.00

Holland & Barrett

Health food shop

Health food shop. This branch has a freezer with vegan ice-cream.

81 Powis Street
Woolwich
London SE18 8LQ

Tel: 020-8316 5490

Mon–Sat:
9.00–17.30,

Sun closed

SOUTH LONDON Wholefood & health food shops

Holland & Barrett

This branch of Holland and Barret health foods has a freezer section and weekly deliveries of fresh take-away food.

68 The Broadway
Wimbledon
London SW19 1RQ

Tel: 020-8542 7486

Mon-Sat: 9.00-17.30,

Holland & Barrett

This branch of the high street chain of heath food shops has a freezer section for those important purchases of vegan ice-cream in South London. They also stock some fresh take- away item like pasties but not sandwiches.

Health food shop

3 Mitcham Rd
Tooting
London SW17 9PA

Tel: 020-8767 8552

Mon-Sat: 9.00-17.30,

Holland & Barrett

Health food shop with lots of veggie snack food.

Health food shop

Unit 19, The
Aylesham Centre
Rye Lane
Peckham
London SE15 5EW

Tel: 020-7639 3354

Mon-Sat: 9.00-17.30,
Sun 11-16.00

Wholefood & health food shops **SOUTH LONDON**

Holland & Barrett

Health food shop

This branch has some fresh take-away and also a freezer section.

137 High St
Putney
London SW15 1SU

Tel: 020–8785 7018

Mon–Sat: 9.00–17.30
Sun: 11.00–15.00

Holland & Barrett

Health food shop

Health foods and wholefoods here but no freezer or take-aways, though plenty of snack foods.

198 Eltham High St
Eltham
London SE9 1TS

Tel: 020–8859 7075

Mon–Sat: 9.30–17.30

Holland & Barrett

Health food shop

Usual range of wholefoods and healtb-foods .

110 Streatham High
Rd., Norbury
London SW16 1BW

Tel: 020–8769 1418

Mon–Sat: 9.00–17.30

SOUTH LONDON Wholefood & health food shops

Holland & Barrett

They have a freezer section here with vegan ice-cream.

Health food shop

67 Riverdale Court
Lewisham
London SE13 7ER

Tel: 020-8297 9559

Mon-Sat: 9.00-17.30
Sun: 10.00-16.00

Holland & Barrett

Regular health food shop.

Health food shop

Unit 6, Surrey Quays
Shopping Ctr
Redriff Road
Surrey Quays
London SE16 1LL

Tel: 020-7231 1043

Mon-Sat: 9.30-18.00
Fri until 20.00,
Sun: 12.00-17.00

Holland & Barrett

Health food shop with plenty of snack foods.

Health food shop

33 Winslade Way
Catford
London SE6 4JU

Tel: 020-8690-3903

Mon-Sat: 9.00-17.30

Natural's Way

There are 2 floors to this health food shop. They have a very large range of foodstuffs on the lower floor, while on the upper floor are supplements, remedies, oils, green products, stationery and cruelty-free cosmetics. People come from a long way to shop here.

There's plenty for vegans including the whole Plamil range. All the take-aways are veggie or vegan and include carrot cutlets and eccles cakes.

The owner gives Indian head massage.

5% discount for Vegetarian Society members.

Formerly called Natural Way.

252 Streatham High Road
Streatham
London SW16 1HS

Tel: 020-8769-0065

Mon-Sat:
9.30-18.30,

Sun closed

People & Planet

Fair trade & veggie food store

Fair trade shop that has been going for 8 years now. Selling mostly traidcraft stock including rice, nuts, dried fruit, pasta, chocolate, speciality teas and coffees. Also veggie Christmas Pud and veggie biscuits.

They have gifts, cards, clothing and aromatherapy oils, as well as Rough Guides books and tapes.

80 Sydenham Road
London SE26 8TY

Tel: 020-8473-7489

Mon-Fri:
8.00-20.00,

Sat: 8.00-18.00,

Sun: 10.00-16.00

SOUTH LONDON Wholefood & health food shops

277

Provender Wholefoods

Friendly wholefood store with pasties, salads and rolls to take away, some books also. They make their own organic bread. Organic fruit and veg arrives Thursdays. There are plans afoot to open a small café within the shop.

103 Dartmouth Road
Forest Hill
London SE23 3HT

Tel: 020-8699-4046

Mon–Sat:
9.00–18.00,

Sun closed

Sheel Pharmacy

Health food shop
& take–away

Not just a pharmacy, they have savoury take-aways and cakes. Wide range of vegan foods and cosmetics.

5% discounts for Vegetarian and Vegan Society members on Thursday.

Chiropodist on the same site.

312–314 Lewisham
Road
Lewisham
London SE14

Tel: 020-8297-1551

Tube:
Lewishham BR

Mon–Fri:
9.00–19.00,

Sat: 9.00–18.00,

Sun closed

SOUTH LONDON

Wholefood & health food shops

Vegetaria

Small wholefood and health food shop with green grocers (not organic).

Wholefood and health food shop

25 Half Moon Lane
Herne Hill
London SE24

Tel: 020-7274-5759

Mon-Sat:
8.00-18.00,

Sun closed

Vitality Health Foods

Health food store inside a shopping centre. No fresh take-away, but plenty of other dried goods and health foods available

Health food shop

Savacentre
1 Merton High Street
London SW19 1DD

Tel: 020-8544-9433

Mon-fri:
9.00-21.00,

Sat: 9.00-20.00,

Sun: 11.00-17.00

SOUTH LONDON Wholefood & health food shops

Well Bean Health Food Shop

Vegan manager here so plenty of vegan grub to be had. Also dried fruits, nuts, seeds, gluten –free range, chilled section has vegan ice-cream. 10% Vegetarian & Vegan Society discount with card.

9 Old Dover Road London SE3

Tel: 020–8858 6854

Mon–Fri:
9.00–18.00

Well Being Foods

Wholefoods and organic shop

Complete selection of wholefoods and organic fruit and veg, plus take-away pies, pasties, salads, fresh breads and some cakes, and a good freezer selection. Body care and household products range.

19 Sydenham Road London SE26 5EX

Tel: 020–8659–2003

Mon–Sat:
9.00–18.00,

Sun closed

Wholefood & health food shops

This new 16-page booklet by the Vegan Society shows how to replace milk and eggs with vegan products, how to make pizza, pancakes and cakes, shop for cruelty-free food, drink, clothes and cosmetics and how to ensure a hassle-free holiday at home or abroad.

Vegans believe that since milk and beef, eggs and chicken all come from the same place, they are all equally unappealing. Now that there is a vegan equivalent to virtually everything, from Cheatin' Ham to chocolate ice-cream, it's never been easier to avoid dairy and egg products, and increasing numbers of vegetarians and even meat eaters are choosing to do just this.

For a copy of Go Vegan, send a cheque or stamps for £1 to The Vegan Society, Donald Watson House, 7 Battle Road, St Leonards-on-Sea, East Sussex, TN37 7AA. www.vegansociety.com Tel 0845-4588 244

Middlesex

Places in Middlesex

Vegetarian restaurants

Wholefood & healthfood shops

MIDDLESEX

A1 Sweet

Popular vegetarian Indian café with good honest food at no frills prices. Family owned for the last 30 years.

13 starters like Dhal Kachori £1.50-2.00.

15 main meals include Masala Dosa or Saag & Makki Roti £2.75-3.50, some of them vegan.

14 desserts £1.50-2.50, but none vegan.

Soft drinks 50p with food.

Indian café

106 The Broadway
Southall
Middlesex UB1 1QF

Tel: 020-8574 2821

Tube:
Southall BR

Tue-Fri:
9.00-18.00,

Sat: 9.00-19.00,

Sun: 10.00-18.00.

Closed Mon.

Ram's Gujarati Surti Cuisine

Indian Gujarati vegetarian cuisine from the city of Surat. Around £8 for a thali with starter such as bhajias, papodoms, two curries, three djipatis, dal and dessert.

They use butter ghee, but vegetable ghee is available.

Desserts include vegan halva. Milkshakes can be made with soya milk.

Licensed. All non-smoking. Wheelchair access and toilet. Visa, MC.

Indian vegetarian restaurant

203 Kenton Road
Kenton
Harrow

Tel: 020-8907 2022

Tube:
Kenton Rd 5 mins

Tue-Sun 12-15.00,
closed Mon

Chetna's

Gujarati and South Indian vegetarian restaurant with take-away service specializing in Indian snacks, dosas, simple curries and pizzas. Affordable food and highly recommended by the Young Indian Vegetarians.

All the usual Indian starters such as bhelpoori, pani poori, dahi bateta poori, or aloo tiki from £2.40.

Plenty of choice of dosas, all under £5, like paper dosa served with vegetable sambhar. If you fancy a change from the usual Indian fare you can also get a large vegetarian deep pan pizza or a hot and spicy one between £5.90 and £6.70 with a choice of toppings and extras.

There is a range of vegetarian desserts but nothing vegan.

Several wines and a selection of beers including Kingfisher.

Minimum charge of £5.50 per person and they now accept cards. High chairs available for weeny veggies.

420 High Road
Wembley
Middlesex HA9 6AH

Tel:
020-8903 5989

Tube:
Wembley Park,
Wembley Central

Mon: closed,
Tue–Fri:
12.00-15.00 and
18-22.30.

Sat–Sun:
13.00-22.30

MIDDLESEX

Vegetarian restaurants

Jashan

Newish Indian vegetarian restaurant aims to "promote healthy vegetarian food, that's rightly spiced and less oily". The menu has 13 different sections and stacks of veggie snacks.

Vegetarian specialities include bharwan bhindi, pakoda kadhi or jeera aloo for £3.50. Then there are 'treasures of the Nawabs': subzi pulao or saade chawal for £2.95 each. "Tangy bites" include aloo tikkiya chaat or karol baug ke samose at £2.95. Mumbai Express section has a Bombay burger for £3.25.

Classics such as veg biriyani are also available here, noodles and of course rice. Lots of Indian breads like paratha, tandoori roti, masala kulchi for around £1.50–£1.95.

Many cold drinks like fresh coconut water and fresh lime juice with soda water.

They have outside seating in the summer for around 25 people. This is an alcohol and smoke free zone.

1-2 Coronet Parade
Ealing Road
Wembley
Middlesex HA0 4AY

Tel: 020-8900-9800

Mon–Fri:
12.00–15.30,
18.00–23.00,

Sat–Sun:
12.00–23.00

MIDDLESEX Vegetarian restaurants

Pradip

Indian vegetarian restaurant and sweet shop next door.

All day buffet Fri–Sun £6.90. As well as a la carte, they plan to introduce a thali for £4.90.

Being next to a sweet shop they're good at desserts, including Lebanese baklava, date rolls, vegan ladhu and coconut sweets.

They use vegetable ghee in cooking and butter ghee in sweets. Not licensed. No smoking. Visa, MC, Diners, Amex. Outside catering service.

*154 Kenton Road
Kenton, Harrow
Middlesex HA3 8AZ*

*Tel: 020-8909 2232
shop 8907 8399
Tube: Kenton Road*

*Restaurant Tue–Sun
12-15.30, 18–22.00*

*Shop
Tue–Sat 10–19.00,
Sun 9–17.00*

closed Mon

*www.pradipsweet.co
.uk*

Maru's Bhajia House

Indian café

Ealing Road has a number of inexpensive Gujarati and south Indian restaurants. Maru's Kenyan Asian cuisine has been a firm favourite for over 20 years with bhajias of course, samosas, maize and assorted snacks.

Asian film stars fill up here on pani puri, kachori and vada. £2.90 for a portion, £5.80 for a double portion.

This is a café and gets very busy at lunchtimes and weekends.

*230 Ealing Road
Alperton
Wembley
Middlesex HA0 4QL*

Tel: 020 8903– 6771

*Tube: Alperton,
Wembley Central*

*Mon–Thurs:
12.30–20.30,*

*Fri–Sun:
12.30–21.30*

*Closed Monday in
summer.*

MIDLLESEX

Vegetarian restaurants

Naklank Sweet Mart

Gujarati vegetarian Indian eat in or take-away. Everything made on the premises with 39 different sweets and savouries, samosas, pakoras, 20 kinds of bhajia.

Curries from £2.50 and mostly vegan. All traditionally made. Small seating area with two tables inside.

Outside catering service.

Gujarati Indian restaurant

50b Ealing Road
Wembley
Middlesex HA0 4TQ

Tel: 020-8902 8008

Tube:

Mon–Sat:
10.00–19.00,

Sun: 11.00–19.00

Natraj

Indian vegetarian take-away with plenty for vegans.

Starters/snacks such as bhajias, sweets, samosas, etc.

Most curries are vegan such as spinach and chickpea, okra and potato, cabbage and potato, soya bean, kidney bean and butterbean mix. A regular take-away box of curry is £2.50, large £3.50. Box of rice £1.50 and £2.50. Or get a box of half curry, half rice for £2 or £3, ideal for lunch.

Indian take-away

341 Northolt Road
South Harrow
Middlesex HA2 8JB

Tel: 020-8426 8903

Tube:
South Harrow

Mon–Tue, Thu–Sat:
10.00–19.30,

closed Wed

Sun 10–16.00

MIDDLESEX Vegetarian restaurants

Sakonis Vegetarian Restaurant

Vegetarian Indian restaurant that also serves lots of Chinese dishes.

Same menu as Wembley, see next page.

Same menu as Wembley, see next page.

Indian & Chinese restaurant

*5-8 Dominion Parade
Station Road
Harrow
Middlesex HA1 2TR*

Tel: 020-8863-3399

*Mon–Sat:
12.00–22.30*

Shahanshah

North Indian vegetarian restaurant, take-away and sweet centre with 50% of their ingredients organic.

Starters £1-1.25 such as two samosas eat in for £1, pakora £1. Main meal £5, eg curry and rice. Vegetarian but not vegan food as they use butter ghee.

Outside seating for 10 people and around 30 inside. Alcohol and smoke-free. No cards. They cater for parties and weddings.

North Indian veggie & vegan restaurant

*60 North Road
Southall
Middlesex UB1 2JL*

Tel: 020-8574-1493

*Tube:
Ealing Broadway,
Southall BR*

*every day
10.00–20.00*

MIDLLESEX

Vegetarian restaurants

Sakonis Vegetarian Restaurant

Vegetarian Indian snack bar, take-away and delivery service with an extensive menu of over 100 Gujarati, North Indian and Chinese dishes. Starters £1.40–£3.95 such as sev puri, pani puri, samosas, toasted sandwiches, spring rolls, khichi or pancake made from gram flour.

Main dishes £2.50–£6.50 such as Mysore masala dosa, farari cutlets, vegetable biriyani, corn bhaji, veggie burger and chips, Manchow soup, chow mein with haka noodles and fried veg, Szechuan spicy noodles, aubergine and chilli in hot black bean sauce.

Lots of sweets, fruit shakes and fresh juices for £2.50.

119–121 Ealing Road
Wembley
Middlesex HA0 4BP

Tel: 020-8903-9601

Tube:
Wembley Central,
Wembley Park

Every day
11.00–22.30

MIDDLESEX Vegetarian restaurants

Supreme Sweets

Indian vegetarian take–away.

Sweets and savouries like bhajias £6 per kilo, samosas and pakoras from 40p. Also a range of frozen products like samosas, kachoris and spring rolls.

75% of the items are vegan, vegetable oil in savouries but butter ghee in sweets. As in many Indian shops no eggs are used.

Catering for weddings and parties, they prepare for you to collect but deliver on orders over 100 people.

706 Kenton Road
Kenton
Harrow
Middlesex HA3 9QX

Tel: 020–8206 2212

Tube: Kingsbury

Mon–Fri:
10.00–19.00,

Sat: 9.30–19.00,

Sun: 8.30–17.30

Woodlands

Indian restaurant

Long established vegetarian Indian restaurant, one of three in London serving classic Indian dishes. This branch is decorated in vibrant colours with a bright and airy feel.
Located within walking distance of Wembley conference centre, and 5 minutes from Wembley Central. This branch has regular changing specials. For more menu details see the Marylebone Road branch (page 82).

402a High Road
Wembley
Middlesex HA9 9LH

Tel: 020–8902 9869

Tube:
Wembley Central,
Wembley Stadium

Mon–Fri:
12.00–15.00 then
18.00–23.00,

Sat–Sun:
12.00–23.00

MIDDLESEX

Vegetarian restaurants

Bodywise Health Foods

Health food shop with focus on complete nutrition and complementary therapies, with health foods, chilled foods, gluten-free, full range of vitamins, supplements, sports nutrition and minerals. Lots of herbal and homeopathic remedies. Their non-food stock includes books, toiletries and cosmetics such as Beauty Without Cruelty range.

There's an in-house complementary therapy clinic with different practitioners visiting daily for reflexology, kineseology, homeopathy and Swedish massage.

249 Station Road
Harrow
Middlesex HA1 2TB

Tel: 020–8861–3336

Mon–Sat:
9.00–18.00,

Sun closed

Food for Thought

Wholefood shop

Wholefood shop with lots of organic food, a wide range of toiletries, BWC cruelty-free cosmetics. They have a take-away section with sandwiches, pies, pasties, salads and burgers, some of which are vegan.

154 High Street
Hounslow
Middlesex TW3 1LR

Tel: 020–8572–0310

Mon–Sat:
9.00–17.30,

Sun closed

MIDLESEX Wholefood & health food shops

Gaia Wholefoods

Wholefood shop selling fresh organic fruit and vegetables, Japanese macrobiotics, organic bread. They stock body care, eco cleaning products and gluten free ranges. Also some vegan take-aways like pastries.

123 St Margarets Road
Twickenham
Middlesex TW1 2LH

Tel: 0181-892 2262

Mon-Fri: 9.30-19.00,
Sat: 17.00,
Sun closed

Holland & Barrett

Health food shop

Fresh veggie take-away snacks like pies and pastries and soyos rolls arrive every Tuesday.

13 King St
Twickenham
Middlesex TW1 3SD

Tel: 020-8891-6696

Mon-Sat: 9.00-17.30,
Sun: closed

Holland & Barrett

Health food shop

Health food shop with a few take-aways like pasties, but no vegan ice-cream.

22-24 College Road
Harrow
Middlesex HA1 1BE

Tel: 020-8427 4794

Mon-Sat: 9.00-17.30,
Sun: closed

Wholefoods& health food shops MIDDLESEX

Holland & Barrett

They have a small take-away section with pastries, plus usual health foods and a chiller cabinet and freezer section.

Unit 21 Wembley Sq.
High Road
Wembley
Middlesex HA9 7AJ

Tel: 020-8902-6959

Mon–Sat:
9.30–17.30,
Sun closed

The Healthy Harvest Food Store

Wholefood shop

Get your gardening goodies and tank up on grub at this wholefood shop (not vegetarian) in a garden centre between Twickenham and Hampton Court. Usual foods plus serve yourself wholefoods.

One variety of fresh veggie pastie available. They no longer stock fresh take-away food as the garden centre has a restaurant.

In Squires Garden
Centre
6 Cross Road
Twickenham
Middlesex TW2 5PA

Tel: 020-8943-0692

Mon–Sat:
9.30–17.30, Sun
from 10.00–17.00

MIDDLESEX Wholefood & health food shops

Places in Surrey

Vegetarian restaurants

Omnivorous restaurants

Wholefood shops

SURREY

by Jo Lacey of Viva!, the vegetarian charity based in Brighton, one of the best cities in the world for vegetarians and vegans.

Hop on the train at Victoria for an awayday or weekend. Mooch around the cutest shops, scoff in veglicious cafes and restaurants, sup in the veggie pub and treat your feet at Vegetarian Shoes. Over 150 entries. Vast accommodation section including comprehensive details of prices, food, vegan options, views, ambience, location and what the rooms are like. Pocket size, 136 pages, indexes, map.

£2.99 + postage from Vegetarian Guides

Also available direct from Viva! 01273-777688
www.viva.org.uk

Richmond Harvest Restaurant

International wholefood vegetarian restaurant using 80% organic ingredients with a small amount of outside seating. The menu clearly marks vegan dishes and those that include nuts, eggs and wheat.

4 of the 7 starters are vegan like tamari mushrooms, soup of the day, hummous with wholemeal bread.

Salads such as white cabbage with horse-radish dressing, or bean with mustard, and tabouleh. Salad combos large £4.95 or small £3.25.

Main courses £5.95, several of them vegan. Try root vegetable crumble topped with oat flakes and sesame seeds; Chinese casserole with ginger and tamari sauce; or butterbean curry with brown rice.

At lunchtimes jacket spuds are available with some of the main dishes as fillings, like butter bean curry for £4.50.

Five desserts and the hot fruit crumble is vegan at £3.25.

Vegetarian and vegan wine £2.50 a glass or £10.95 a bottle. Beer £2.95. A 10% service charge applies after 5pm and cards are accepted.

International restaurant

5 The Square
Richmond
Surrey TW9 1DT

Tel: 020-8940 1138

Tube:
Richmond BR

Mon–Sun:
11.30–23.00

SURREY Vegetarian restaurants

Riverside Vegetaria

Superb riverside vegetarian restaurant with large windows that open out over the Thames. It is particularly idyllic in summer but well worth the trip out to Kingston at any time of year. In warm weather you can eat under the sky in the outdoor area on the towpath beside the river. 70% vegan including some awesome desserts.

Starters £3.95–£4.30 like potato balls with chilli sauce, sweet potato soup, garlic mushrooms, and falafel.
Main dishes £5.50–£6.70 include masala dosa; string hopper biriyani with fine noodles; tofu marinated in teriyaki sauce, mushroom and lentil bake; all served with veg, salad and/or rice.
A truly great vegetarian restaurant is memorable for its desserts and vegans especially will never forget Riverside Vegetaria after scoffing some of the vegan desserts like chocolate cake or baked figs with orange and brandy. They even have soya custard. From £2.95.
Lots of soft drinks, liquor, Ginseng beer and even champagne from £26.95. Organic wines and Disos vegan red and white.

Discounts for Vegetarian and Vegan Society members and clever people presenting this book! Booking advised a couple of days ahead for weekends and outside. Take-away including frozen soup by the litre. Outside catering. Families and parties welcome.

64 High Street
Kingston-upon-Thames
Surrey

Tel: 020-8546 7992

Tube: Kingston BR

Every day:
12.00–23.00.

SURREY

Vegetarian restaurants

Santok Maa's

North and South Indian vegetarian restaurant and take-away, with some Chinese dishes that use Indian spices like stir-fries.

Nearly 100 veggie and vegan dishes. Starters average £2.95, main courses £3.95, rice £1.75.

Desserts from £1.50 but no vegan ones.

Bring your own wine, £1 per person corkage.

Special offer on Monday, all food half price excluding dessert and take-away.

Visa, MC, Amex. Outside catering for weddings and parties. Eggless cakes.

North and South
Indian restaurant

848 London Road
Thornton Heath
Surrey CR7 7PA

Tel: 020-8665-0626

Tube:
Thornton Heath BR,
Norbury BR

Thu–Tue:
12.00–22.00.

Closed Wed.

SURREY Vegetarian restaurants

Tide Tables

Vegetarian café under the arch of a bridge near the town centre, with beautiful views of the Thames, a riverside terrace and outside seating in summer. All food is GM free and menu items are clearly marked up for gluten-free, organic and vegan.

The breakfast menu offers organic muesli, toasted organic muffin with jam, almond croissants or pain chocolat from £1.35 to £2.50.

For lunch and tea there's vegan soup, spinach pastie with salad, stuffed focaccia, vegan shepherdess pie with salad, falafel, from £2.20 to £5.90.

Handmade organic cakes, but none appeared to be vegan. Hot and cold drinks and free corkage.

Child and dog friendly and a nice place to meet friends for lunch. Phone ahead first for opening hours if visiting in deepest darkest winter.

Vegetarian café

2 The Archways
Richmond Bridge
Richmond
Surrey TW9 1TH

Tel: 020-8948-8285

Tube:
Richmond BR

Open daylight hours, phone ahead as they close if weather is bad

Veggie One

Vegetarian
Chinese restaurant

322 Limpsfield Road
Sanderstead
South Croydon
Surrey CR2 9BX

Tel: 020-8651-1233

Tube:
Sanderstead train

Tues-Sun:
18.00-23.00,

closed Mon

Vegetarian Chinese restaurant and take-away, GM free and completely organic. All their dishes are vegan except the egg fried rice. Evening meal £10-15 per person.

For starters try crispy aromatic duck, tempura vegetables, crispy fruit roll in rice paper, deep fried tofu Thai style or dim-sum at £1.80-£6.00.

Mains £2.00-£5.50 include aubergine and bean casserole, vegan pork, vegan fish, abalone mushrooms with sesame.

8 desserts £2.00-3.50 such as toffee apple, toffee banana, mango pancake, fresh fruit, fruit cocktail, lychees, banana or pineapple fritter.

They want to promote health, so though licensed they don't sell alcohol and it's smoke free. But you can bring your own drinks. Non alcoholic wine £5.50 or £6 per bottle, non-alcoholic beer £1.50 or £2, soft drinks and soya milk.

Cheques or cash, no credit cards. They have a wholesale vegetarian frozen food business called Vegetarian Paradise. Croydon and Sutton Vegans sometimes meet here.

Stop press for 2003: organic wine now available.

Wagamama

Omnivorous fast food Japanese noodle bar with over nine veggie and vegan dishes. See Bloomsbury, WC1 branch for details.

www.wagamama.com

16–18 High Street
Kingston-upon-
Thames
Surrey KT1 1EY

Tel: 020–8546 1117

Tube:
Kingston BR

Mon–Sat:
11.00–23.00,

Sun: 12.30–22.30

Omnivorous restaurants SURREY

Food for Thought

Wholefood shop with plenty of staples like dried fruit, nuts, seeds, pulses etc. plus supplements, aromatherapy, skin-care ranges, and homeopathic remedies.

Wholefoods shop

38 Market Place
Kingston
Surrey KT1 1JQ

Tel: 020-8546-7806

TMon-Sat:
9.00-17.30,

Sun closed

Holland & Barrett

The frozen and chilled counter is well stocked but there's no fresh take-away at this store.

Health food shop

Unit 44,
Ashley Centre
Epsom
Surrey

Tel: 01372-728520

Mon-Sat:
9.00-17.30,

Sun: 10.00-16.00

Holland & Barrett

Have limited fresh take–away like pies and pasties, some vegan. Also frozen/chilled section.

213 High Street
Sutton
Surrey SN1 1LB

Tel: 020–8642–5435

Mon–Sat: 9.00–17.30,
Sun: 11.00–16.00

Holland & Barrett

One of the larger stores with fresh take–away snacks, a big chilled and frozen section, supplements and toiletries.

Health food shop

1098–99 The Mall
Whitgift Centre
Croydon
Surrey CR0 1UU

Tel: 020–8681 5174

Mon–Sat: 9.00–18.00,
Thur: 9.00–20.00,
Sat: 8.30–18.30,
Sun: 11.00–17.00

Holland & Barrett

Fresh take–away snacks available, some of which may be vegan like pasties and pies. There is a chiller section and frozen food.

Health food shop

12–13 Apple Market
Kingston
Surrey KT1 1JF

Tel: 020–8541–1378

Mon–Fri: 9.00–17.30,
Sat: 9.00–18.00,
Sun: 11.00–16.30

Wholefood & health food shops **SURREY**

Holland & Barrett

Fresh take-away snacks as well as the usual health foods and supplements.

50a George St
Richmond
Surrey TW9

Tel: 020-8940 1007

Mon–Sat:
9.00–17.30,

Sun: 11.30–16.30

Oliver's Wholefood

Wholefood shop

Wholefood shop with a wide selection of produce, not all of it veggie. Good location next to the tube station and handy for picking up something to nibble while you visit Kew Gardens.

5 Station Approach
Kew Gardens
Richmond
Surrey TW9 3QB

Tel: 020-8948 3990

Veggie and vegan take-away snacks include sandwiches, pastries, salads, seaweed rice and wraps. They sell vegan wines as well as organic fruit and veg.

Tube:
Kew Gardens

Mon–Sat:
9.00–19.00,

Sun: 10.00–19.00

The store has a trained nutritionist and beauty therapist on site for advice and there are regular lectures in-store on topics like living food and digestive health.

SURREY Wholefood & health food shops

Vegetarian
Ethnic eating

One third of the people living in London are not English. The availability of vegetarian and vegan food in London owes a great deal to the diverse communities which have had a massive impact on British eating habits. Here we give a brief overview of London's ethnic communities and their offerings for the vegetarian gastronome when out shopping, or late night when clean living veggie restaurants may be shut.

CARIBBEAN

What:
breadfruit, ackee, limes, mangoes, guavas, yams, sweet potato, callalloo, plantain, chirstophene, pumpkin, green bananas, creamed coconut, cassava.

Shopping:
Shops in Brixton, Hackney, Harlesden, Notting Hill

Markets:
Brixton, SW2
Shepherds Bush, between Uxbridge and Goldhawk Road, W12
Ridley Road, Dalston, E8
Northcote Road, Battersea, SW11
Rye Lane, Peckham, SE15

Try this at home:
Caribbean Cookery for Vegans, 52 exotic recipes from one of the world's most exciting culinary regions. Send a cheque for £3 to Two Sevens, 30 Wynter Street, London SW11 2TZ.

GREEK, TURKISH & CYPRIOT

What:
Hummous, aubergines, beans, vine leaves, olive oil, Mediterrean vegetables, sticky sweets and cakes.

Shopping:
Finsbury Park, Green Lanes, Hackney, Stoke Newington

Where:
Kalamaras, 66 Inverness Mews, Bayswater W2 (Greek)
Lemonia, 89 Regents Park Road, NW1 (Greek)
Sofra cafes and restaurants in central London (Turkish)
Tas, 33 The Cut, Waterloo, SE1 (Turkish)
Tadim Cafe & Bakery, 41 Camberwell Church St, SE5 (Turkish)

CHINESE

What:
Rice, noodles, soy sauce, spices, water chestnuts, bamboo shoots, mooli, lotus root, tofu (beancurd), tempeh, wheat gluten (seitan), fake meat, Jasmine tea.

Shopping:
Supermarkets in Chinatown, sandwiched between Leicester Square and Shaftesbury Avenue.

Chinese vegetarian restaurants:
Chai, 236 Station Road, Edgware
Chi, 55 St Martin's Lane, WC2 (Leicester Square tube)
CTJ, 339 Euston Road, NW1(Warren St, Great Portland St)
CTV, 22 Golder's Green Road (Golder's Green)
Joi, 14 Percy Street, W1 (Goodge Street)
Kai, 244 West Hendon Broadway, NW9
Peking Palace, 669 Holloway Road, N19 (Archway)
SASA, 13 Islington High Street, N1 (Angel)
SASA, 271 Muswell Hill Broadway, N10
Sayur Mayur, 87 Battersea Rise, SW11 (Clapham Junction BR)
Tai, 10 Greek Street, W1 (Soho)
Vegan Thai Buffet, 167 The Vale, W3 (Acton)
Veggie One, 322 Limpsfield Rd, South Croydon, Surrey

INDIAN SUBCONTINENT

What:
Dosa (large stuffed pancake), bhajia, samosa, iddlies (steamed rice cakes) spicy vegetable savouries, rice, chutneys, okra, pulses, peas, spinach, thali combination dish

Shopping: Wembley (Gujarati), Southall (Sikh and Bengali)

Central Indian vegetarian restaurants:
Brick Lane, E1, has 20 omnivorous tandoori restaurants.
Chutneys, Diwana & Ravi Shankar in Drummond Street, NW1
Indian Veg, Chapel Market, N1 (Angel)
Rasa, Dering Street, W1 (Bond Street)
Sagar, 157 King Street, Hammersmith
Vegetarian Paradise, 59 Marchmont St, Bloomsbury
Woodlands, 37 Panton Street (Leicester Sq, Piccadilly Circus)

ITALIAN

What:
Mediterranean vegetables, sun-dried tomatoes, olives, artichokes, ciabatta bread, olive oil, garlic, herbs, pasta, pizza.

West End Italian cafes and restaurants:
Frith Street, Compton Street, Old Compton Street, Moor Street, Charlotte Street.

JAPANESE

What:
Miso soup, sushi (rice and veg in nori seaweed rolls), ramen rice noodles, udon buckwheat noodles, soba wheat noodles, tofu, daikon raddish, pickled ginger, green tea, sake.

Central Shopping:
Brewer Street area, W1, has Japanese shops.
The two Planet Organic and six Fresh & Wild wholefood super-markets sell many Japanese foods.

Central restaurant chains:
Wagamama, Ikkyu, Moshi-Moshi, Tsukuba.

LATIN AMERICA

What:
Corn, beans, chillis, sweetcorn, avocado, tomatoes, lemon, lime, exotic fruits and spices, burritos, fajitas, chimichangas, tacos, guacamole, sweet potatoes, beer, tequila, cocktails, party atmosphere.

Mexican and Cuban restaurants:
Acapulco, 219 Finchley Road, NW3
Cuba Libre, 72 Upper Street, N1
Havana, 490 Fulham Road, SW6
Texas Embassy Cantina, 1 Cockspur Street, SW1.

JEWISH

What:
Hummous, falafels, bagels, *parve* (meat and dairy free) ice cream, biscuits, chocolate, cakes, "cream cheese", margarine.

Shopping and restaurants:
Golders Green Road

More information:
Jewish Vegetarian Society, 853–855 Golders Green Rd, NW11 8LX. Tel 020–8455 0692. Publishes a quarterly magazine, talks and social events, cookery courses.

MALAYSIAN AND INDONESIAN

What:
Exotic vegetables, fuits, nuts, tempeh, satay (peanut butter sauce), rice, noodles, mango.

Where:
Melati, 30 Peter Street, W1 and 21 Great Windmill St, W1
The Satay Bar, 447 Coldharbour Lane, SW9
Shamsudeen's, 35 & 119 Stoke Newington Church St, N16
Silks & Spice, 28 Chalk Farm Road, NW1;
    95 Chiswick High Road, W4; 23 Foley Street, W1;
    The Arcade, Liverpool St, EC2; 42 Northampton Rd, EC1
VitaOrganic, 279c Finchley Road (vegan)

LEBANESE

What:
Hummous, chickpeas, couscous, tahini, aubergines, garlic, lemon, crushed wheat, olive oil, olives, garlic, beans, rice.

Where:
Byblos, 262 Kensington High St, W8
Gaby's, 30 Charing Cross Road, WC2

SPANISH

What:
Tapas snacks like chilli potatoes, spinach and pine nuts, spiced green beans, olives, nuts, spiced mushrooms

Where:
The Finca, 96 Pentonville Rd, N1
and 185 Kennington Lane, SE11
The Gallery Restaurant, 76 Parry Street, SW8
Meson Don Felipe, wine and tapas bar, 53A The Cut, SE1

THAI

What:
Bean curd, sticky rice, wild rice, noodles, yellow and black bean sauces, seaweed, crispy vegetables, lemon grass, limes, ginger, banana leaf, coconut milk, hot chillies, peanut sauce, lychees, papaya

Restaurants:
Thai Garden, 249 Globe Road, Bethnal Green, E2
Blue Elephant, 4 Fulham Broadway, SW6
Sri Siam, 16 Old Compton St, W1
Sri Siam, 85 London Wall, EC2
Yum Yum Express, 30 Stoke Newington Church St, N16
Mantanah, 2 Orton Buildings, Portland Rd, SE25

Mail order ethnic veggie cookbooks:

The Vegan Society catalogue, send an sae to 7 Battle Road, St Leonards-on-Sea, East Sussex TN37 7AE. 0845-45 88244. www.vegansociety.com

Viva! Books for Life catalogue, 12 Queen Square, Brighton BN1 3FD. 01273-777 688. www.viva.org.uk

Central London bookshops have big foodie sections with shelves groaning with veggie cookbooks. For some superb and hard to find American vegan cookbooks try **Borders** in Oxford Street (just east of Oxford Circus, till 11pm) or at the top of Charing Cross Road. In these two stores you can read books for free on the comfy sofas in the store or take them to the cafes which serve soya cappuccino until 9pm.

Some health food and wholefood stores have book sections, for example **Planet Organic** (W2 and Bloomsbury), **Fresh and Wild** (six branches), **Revital Health Place** (Victoria, Sloane Zone).

Accommodation

Barrow House

Bed & breakfast

Vegetarian and vegan bed and breakfast in south London, in a Victorian family house in a quiet location,.15 minutes by rail from Victoria Station,

Three double/twin rooms, £50 double or £35 single.

Breakfast features fruit salad, cereal, toast, soya margarine and milk always available and even soya yogurt if they know you're coming.

Two vegetarian restaurants and a wholefood store nearby.

45 Barrow Road
Streatham Common
London SW16 5PE

Tel:
020–8677 1925

Fax:
020–8677 1925

Tube:
Streatham Common
British Rail and
close to the A23

Open:
All Year Round

Dora Rothner
Bed and Breakfast

Homely bed and breakfast in North London, where they're used to doing vegetarian or vegan breakfasts as Dora the owner doesn't eat meat.

2 doubles (not twins) and 1 single for £18 per person per night, including breakfast. TV in rooms. Shared bathroom.

Soya milk and margarine always available.

No smoking or pets and only children over twelve.

Handy for Finchley Central tube (Northern line), the North Circular Road and M1.

Rani Indian vegetarian restaurant close by.

They are open all year round including at Christmas and don't charge a single person supplement.

Bed & breakfast

23 The Ridgeway
Finchley
London N3 2PG

Tel:
020–8346 0246

Tube:
Finchley Central

Open:
All year round

Hampstead Village Guesthouse

Veggie friendly 1872 Victorian guest house in a peaceful setting close to the heath and tube. In the heart of lively Hampstead Village, a fun area with art cinema, restaurants with veggie food, coffee shops and pubs. The large, very comfortable rooms are full of character with sitting area, writing desk, remote control TV, hairdryer, iron, fridge (brilliant for veggies), kettle, telephone, books and even a hot-waterbottle to cuddle.

En suite double £84, en suite single £66. Double £72, singles £48 and £54. Large studio with kitchen and shower £90 for 1, £120 for 2, £138 for 3, £150 for 4, £162 for 5. Parking £10 per day.

Optional breakfast £7 from 8.00 a.m., 9.00 at weekends until late, can be in the garden in summer and you can invite guests.

Booking requires credit card, pay on arrival in cash, sterling (travellers) cheques or credit card (5% surcharge). No smoking anywhere. No meals except breakfast, but there are veggie restaurants and a wholefood store in the area and veggie dishes in other nearby restaurants.

www.HampsteadGuesthouse.com
info@HampsteadGuesthouse.com

Veggie friendly hotel

2 Kemplay Road
Hampstead
London NW3 1SY

Tel:
020–7435 8679
Fax:
020–7794 0254

Tube:
Hampstead

5 rooms from
£48–66 single,

£72 upwards for double

HAMPSTEAD VILLAGE GUESTHOUSE

2 Kemplay Road, Hampstead
London NW3 1SY

www.hampsteadguesthouse.com
tel: +44 (0)20 7435 8679 **Fax:** +44 (0)20 7794 0254
e-mail: info@hampsteadguesthouse.com

- Peaceful setting, close to Hampstead Heath, yet in the heart of lively Hampstead Village.

- Close to underground and bus. Centre of London in 10 minutes.

- Large rooms full of character, plus modern amenities: TV, kettle and direct-dial telephone.

- breakfast in the garden, weather permitting.

- Accomodation from £48.

- No smoking.

"If you're looking for something a little different, make a beeline for Annemarie van der Meer's Hampstead home."
Chosen as one of the "Hotels of the Year". The Which? Hotel Guide 2000.

Liz Heavenstone's Guest House

Guest house

Cosy, top floor apartment in a Regency terrace in Primrose Hill village, on the edge of Regent's Park. Two double/twin rooms, £50-60 per room per night, one with own bathroom, one with shower, which become a self contained apartment with living room when both rooms are taken. There's also a futon for an extra bed in one room. Good for self-catering as the double comes with a fridge and microwave with oven.

Add £5 for self-service vegetarian organic breakfast, which can easily be veganized, and they'll happily cater for special diets if you tell them in advance. There are always tea, coffee and herbal drinks, and the breakfast room has a bowl of fruit.

Children welcome but no pets. Discreet smokers tolerated.

They have plenty of info on London for guests. Primrose Hill, Regents Park, Manna vegetarian restaurant, Cafe Seventy Nine and some wholefood stores are nearby. Two minutes walk to Chalk Farm underground. Prior telephone booking is essential, do not just turn up.

heavenstone@btinternet.com

192 Regents Park Road
Hampstead
London NW1 8XP

Tel:
020-7722 7139
Fax:
020-7586 3004

Tube:
Chalk Farm

Open:
All year

Stay with us in Primrose Hill, London NW1

Quiet, charming, friendly apartment
on top two floors of Regency Terrace

Primrose Hill "village" is known for its
cafes, restaurants, parks and central location.
An ideal base from which to explore all that
London has to offer!

£55 or £65 per night per room

Tel: 020-7722 7139 or Fax 020-7586 3004
e-mail: heavenstone@btinternet.com

Quaker International Ctr

Accommodation set within this International Quaker Centre for Christians, near Euston station. Open to all, a single is £34, 3-4 person dorms £20 per person, or twins for £57, including cold continental veggie breakfast.

Basic cooking facilities, microwave plus fridge, and a small snack bar.

Nearby places to eat or shop in Bloomsbury and Fitzrovia include Vegetarian Paradise Indian restaurant, CTJ and Joi Chinese vegan restaurants, Planet Organic cafe and shop, Alara Wholefoods, and Drummond Street with lots of Indian food.

The centre is for hire for group or organisation meetings.

Bed and breakfast

1-3 Byng Place
London WC1E 7JH

Tel:
020-7387 548

Tube:
Euston, Warren Street

Open:
All Year
except Christmas
through to New
Year

Stephanie Rothner Bed and Breakfast

Bed and breakfast

Newish vegetarian homely bed and breakfast, her mum runs the one in N3.

1 single and 1 double at £16 per person per night including breakfast. Shared bathroom. Veggie breakfast with soya milk and margarine always available.

Children over twelve only. No smoking or pets. Two friendly resident cats. They don't charge single person supplement.

44 Grove Road
North Finchley
London N12 9DY

Tel:
020–8446 1604
Mobile:
07956–406446

Tube:
Woodside Park then
15 min walk or
Finchely bus
terminal

Open:
All year round

Temple Lodge

Bed and breakfast

Large Georgian house with garden run by The Christian Community offering bed and breakfast accommodation. 2 singles £25, 3+ nights £22, £150 week. 4 twins £35, £210 week, which can be let as singles at the single rate. Washbasins in rooms. No TV. Continental vegetarian breakfast but vegans must request ahead. Classy vegetarian restaurant The Gate at same address. Close to the Thames and Olympia or Earls Court Exhibition Centres. Underground connection to the West End. No smoking in the house. An oasis of tranquility in a busy city.

51 Queen Caroline Street
Hammersmith
London W6 9QL

Tel:
020–8748 8388
Fax:
020–8748 8322

Tube:
Hammersmith

Open:
All year

The Lanesborough

Luxury hotel popular with veggie rock and movie stars and C.E.O.'s. Singles £265–£275, doubles £370–£395 up to the royal suite for £3500, all plus VAT.

If a veggie/vegan breakfast is required you have to give prior notice at the time of booking. Services include 24 hour butler, fitness studio, health club membership, business suite with Internet/e-mail and computer facilities included in your room with a free video library.

The in-house restaurant The Conservatory features gourmet vegetarian dinners, prepared by top chef Paul Gayler or one of his brigade of 40 chefs. Lunch is £22.50 for 2 courses or £27.50 for three, dinner prices depend on the day of the week but usually range from £32–£44 per head. The vegetarian a la carte menu often has vegan options but not always so phone ahead. There is live music every night and dancing on Friday and Saturday nights.

www.rosewood-hotels.com

Luxury hotel

Hyde Park Corner
Knightsbridge
London SW1X 7TA

Tel:
020–7259 5599
Fax:
020–7259 5606

Tube:
Hyde Park Corner

For reservations in
USA call toll free
1 800 999 1828,
fax: 1–800 937 8278

All over London
Other accommodation

If you're planning on foraging outside and just want a very cheap roof over your head, there are numerous private hostels and bargain bed and breakfasts near the West End in Paddington, W2, (north of Hyde Park), Victoria and Pimlico, King's Cross, South Kensington and Earl's Court, otherwise known as Kangaroo Valley being packed out with Australians and Kiwis on working holidays, from £10 per night depending on length of stay. Find them in the London Tourist Information Board, the accommodation section of free travellers' magazines in pavement dispensers around central London such as *TNT, Southern Cross* and *LAM.* If you're not already in London, our favourite guidebooks for budget places are Lonely Planet, Rough Guides or Let's Go London, England, Britain or Europe. Or go to the fabulous site **www.hostels.com**. If you've just got off a coach or airport train at Victoria station, there are some accommodation agencies that can sort out your first night's stay for a small commission.

Youth Hostels Association members can stay at one of London's eight youth hostels, including City, Earls Court, Hampstead, Highgate, King's Cross/St Pancras, Oxford Street, though watch out for higher prices (around £20) than elsewhere in the country, single sex dorms and possible curfews.

If you're moving to London for at least six months, advertise free for a flatshare or sublet in LOOT, the free ads paper from newsagents, and let the landlords come to you. (www.loot.com) You can repeat the ad every two days. Getting an apartment in London is a full time job for a few days but it can be done if you're persistent. They are expensive, but if you're on a working holiday and pack it with friends, it works out cheaper than a hostel in the long run and much quieter. A single or double room in a houseshare will be £70-120 per week, a studio flat £100 per week and up. You'll need a month's deposit, a month's rent up front, and the contract will normally be a six months assured shorthold tenancy. So staying in a hostel for the first few weeks is definitely a lot less hassle while you find a job and you can get some mates there.

Here are a few hostels to get you started. Call ahead to reserve.

HOSTELS

The Palace Hotel

48–49 Princes Square, Bayswater, London W2 4PX
Email: info-palacehotel@quista.net

Tel: 020-7221 5628
Fax: 020-7 221 5890
Price: £12

On the north side of Hyde Park. Open 24 hours.

Generator Hostel

Compton Place, off 37 Tavistock Place, London
WC1H 9SD
Email: info@the-generator.co.uk
Web: www.the-generator.co.uk

Tel: 020-7388 7666
Fax: 020-7388 7644
Price: £15

Huge tourist hostel with 800 beds at Russell Square in
Bloomsbury. Fantastic location and great facilities. Open 24 hours.

St. Christopher's Inn Camden

48–50 Camden High Street, London 1NP
Tube: Camden Town
Email: bookings@st-christophers.co.uk
Web: www.st-christophers.co.uk

Tel: 020-7407 1856
Fax: 020-7403 7715
Price: £12-13

Near Camden Market, which is brilliant at weekends, 44 bed hostel in a
cool, young area with lots of nightlife.

St. Christopher's Inn South Bank

121 Borough High Street, London SE1 1HR
Tube: London Bridge
Email: bookings@st-christophers.co.uk
Web: www.st-christophers.co.uk

Tel: 020-7407 1856
Fax: 020-7403 7715
Price: £12-13

Party atmosphere hostel with a bar, handy for the City.

North London Backpackers

1st Floor, Queens Parade, Queens Road, Hendon
London NW4
Tube: Hendon Central
Email: info@ukhostel.com

Tel: 020-8203 1319
Fax: 020-8203 9339

International Students House

229 Great Portland Street, London W1N 5HD
Tube: Great Portland Street
Open: All Year,
Reservations phone 020-7631 8310

Tel: 020-7631 8300
Fax: 020-7631 8315

Long term accomodation for students, with dorms. Twin dorm £25 per person per night, 4-person dorm £18, which includes breakfast and they have cooked veggie breakfast options. There's a Chinese all-you-can-eat vegan restaurant for £4.99 nearby, see Marylebone and Fitzrovia section.

YHA HOSTELS

City of London Youth Hostel
36 Carter Street, London EC4V 5AB
Email: city@yha.org.uk

Tel: 020-7236 4965
Fax: 020-7236 7681

Earls Court Youth Hostel, 38 Bolton Gardens
London SW5 0AQ
Email: earlscourt@yha.org.uk

Tel: 020-7373 7083
Fax: 020-7835 2034

Hampstead Heath Youth Hostel
4 Wellgarth Road, Golders Green, London NW11 7HR
Email: hampstead@yha.org.uk

Tel: 020-8458 9054
Fax: 020-8209 0546

Oxford Street Youth Hostel
14 Noel Street, London W1V 3PD
Email: oxfordst@yha.org.uk

Tel: 020-7734 1618
Fax: 020-7734 1657

Rotherhithe Youth Hostel
20 Salter Road, London SE16 1PP
Email: rotherhithe@yha.org.uk

Tel: 020-7232 2114
Fax: 020-7237 2919

CAMPING

Crystal Palace Campsite

Crystal Palace Campsite
Crystal Palace Parade, London SE19
Tube: Crystal Palace BR

Tel: 020–8778 7155
Open all year round

This is a caravan park so electricity is available but no shop or cooking facilities. They do have laundry and washing facilities though. Rates vary according to the time of year. Average is £2.50 per tent, then £3.75 per adult in winter rising to £4.50 adult in summer. Car and tent is £3.50.

Lee Valley Park

Pickets Lock Centre, London N9
Tube: Tottenham Hale or Edmonton BR
Open: All Year Round except Xmas Day, Boxing Day
& New Year

Tel: 020–8803 6900

Huge well equipped site set in 6 acres with sports centre and leisure complex with 12 screen cinema, swimming pool, golf course, kids' play area, 3 pubs and pizza restaurant. Acts as bus terminal for those going into town. There is a minimum charge for everyone £5.65 for adult or £2.35 for children 5–16, for individuals this goes up to £8.00 (i.e. one person and tent). Electricity is £2.40 per night. No charge for dogs or awnings. Another site is nearby at Sewardstone Road, Chingford, E4 7RA Tel 020–8529 5689, closed in winter.

Tent City Acton

Old Oak Common Lane, Acton, London W3
Tube: East Acton
Open: May –Oct 24 hours

Tel: (020) 87435708

Price: £5

Bunk beds in large dorm tents, or bring your own. Prices start at £5 per person. Showers, toilets, basic snack bar.

Tent City Hackney

Millfields Road, Hackney, London E5 OAR
Tube: No. 38 bus to Clapton Pond
Open: May– October

Tel: 020–8985 7656
Fax: 020–898 7656

3 large dormitories in tents with bunk beds. Separate and mixed dorms. Prices start around £5 per person, Under 5's free. Snack bar with salad, sandwiches and fruit open 8-12.00 then 19.00-22.00. Free cooking facilities, on site entertainment, free hot showers, laundry, valuables lock-up, no curfew. Canalside pubs nearby. Profits go to charity.

332

Veggie & vegan catering

Many of the restaurants in this book do outside catering, and this is indicated in the text.

Overleaf are some restaurants that we know have been catering for weddings, parties and events for years, plus some great independent caterers like Leon Lewis (the best veggie catering we've ever seen), Veggies (specialise in demos and animal rights events) and Kat Lubar's vegan cakes.

Barty's Creative Catering

83 Stanley Gardenens, Teddington,   *Tel: 020–8977 9064*
Middlesex TW 11 8SY

Vegetarian and vegan catering service who will cater for any event,
weddings parties, and especially charity events and conferences.

Gannets Vegetarian Café

Hornbeam Environmental Centre, 458 Hoe Street,   *Tel: 020–8558 6880*
Walthamstow, London E17 9AH

Outside catering from one cake to buffets and picnic food for 1,000.

Leon's Vegetarian Catering

132b London Road, Brentwood, Essex CM14 4NS   *Tel: 01277–218661*

Vegetarian and vegan catering, buffets, cookery demonstrations, any event
nationwide.

Naklank

50b Ealing Road, Wembley, Middlesex HAO 4TQ

Indian sweet shop and restaurant catering for parties and weddings.

Tel: 020–8902 8008

Raw Deal

65 York Street, off Seymour Place,   *Tel: 020–7262–4841*
London W1H 1PQ   *Fax 01732–840570*

Veggie café that does part time veggie/vegan catering, phone the café
first and speak to Sandra or Orlando. No deliveries, customer must collect.

Vegan Cakes

E-mail katlubar@aol.com   Tel 020-7243 8225
Mobile daytime 0771-2006983

Part time vegan cake maker, will make cakes to order both novelty and
traditional designs for all occasions. No deliveries, must be collected.

Vegetarian Express

David Jonas, Unit 46, WENTA business Centre,   Tel: 01923-249 714
Cole Way, Watford, Herts WD2 4NP

Wholefooods and organic produce and a range of prepared meals.

Veggies Catering Campaign

The Sumac Centre, 245 Gladstone Street,   Tel: 0845-458 9595
Nottingham NG7 6HX
Email: info@veggies.org.uk
Website www.veggies.org.uk

Part of a large resource centre, Veggies does veggie and vegan catering
nationwide for various events, organisations and charities.   They also run
a café and food stall in the local market as well as veggie cooking lessons
in Nottingham.

Wild Cherry

241 Globe Road, Bethnal Green. London E2 0JD   Tel: 020-8980 6678

Vegetarian Buddhist group that run a café and do outside catering.

ANIMAL FREE
SHOPPER
by The Vegan Society (UK) - 320 pages

Essential for living or travelling in Britain. Indispensable shopping guide to products which are free of animal ingredients and involve no animal testing. Sections include food, drink, footwear, toiletries, cosmetics, remedies, baby & child care, animal care, garden and leisure, home and office, chocolate. Lists additives, mail order addresses, vegan contacts, glossary of animal substances. GM-free products highlighted.

£4.99 + postage from Vegetarian Guides
See order form at the end of this guide or
www.vegetarianguides.co.uk
Or order direct from the Vegan Society (+44) 0845-45 88244
www.vegansociety.com

Ronny's Top Tips
for restaurateurs

The vegan population is growing rapidly, much faster than vegetarianism, and awareness about food allergies and cholesterol is also increasing. Therefore a very significant number of your customers will be actively avoiding eggs and dairy products as well as meat. If you make sure that many of your meals are completely animal free, you will tap into a significant market. Here are some suggestions:

1. There are numerous brands of vegetarian **sausages, burgers and bacon substitutes**. All are quite similar, but some brands contain egg. If you always buy egg-free ones, you will be able to cater for both vegetarians and vegans at the same time. For a total vegan breakfast feast, offer scrambled (mashed and lightly fried) **tofu** as an alternative to scrambled eggs.

2. Always have **soya milk.** It keeps for over a year unopened and up to 5 days when opened. **Soya dessert** and **soya cream** also keep for a long time. Soya milk makes excellent cappuccinos and is perfect for making custard and rice puddings.

3. Try serving **Tofutti** or **Swedish Glace** or **Provamel** ice cream, either on its own or to accompany hot pies and puddings. Just try it and you won't need any further convincing!

4. **Soya cheese** can be used to create some amazing vegan dishes, yet is rarely used in catering. It is easily available pre-packed at wholefood stores, or in bulk blocks from manufacturers and wholesalers. Redwood Foods make a very popular brand called 'Cheezley'. It has a longer shelf life than dairy cheese, even after you open it. Or make your own using *The Uncheese Cookbook* by Joanne Stepaniak, from The Vegan Society, www.vrg.org, amazon.com, or ask at your bookshop.

5. Vegan salads are easy to prepare. **Egg-free mayonnaise** is available in small jars from wholefood stores or buy the excellent Plamil brand in bulk tubs from wholesalers. Alternatively make your own mayonnaise-style dressing by blending vegetable oil with roughly equal quantities of vinegar and soya milk. You could also offer a **vinaigrette** made with olive oil, herbs, mustard and lemon juice or vinegar. If you make up a big batch of this, it will keep for weeks, just shake before serving.

6. **Vegan dips** are no problem. You can easily buy or make hummous, and guacamole can be made just as well without yogurt. Try roasting aubergines and liquidising with olive oil and black pepper for a very rich and creamy baba ganoush dip.

7. For an uncooked **vegan breakfast**, serve a muesli that doesn't have honey or whey in it, or offer toast, crumpets or muffins with vegan margarine. Most brands of vegetable margarine are not vegan as they contain whey powder, but virtually all supermarkets stock at last one vegan brand. Catering size tubs can be bought from wholesalers.

8. Avoid glazing **pastries** with egg, and make sure that the pastry itself as well as the contents are vegan. Bulk packs of frozen puff, filo and shortcrust pastry are widely available from wholesalers.

9. Aim to make **at least half your starters and main courses vegan**. If only one out of four or six options is vegan we don't have any choice. Cheese, cheese or cheese isn't much of a choice for veggies either.

10. It is very frustrating that so many restaurants offer a choice of vegan starters and main courses, but no **dessert**. When there is a dessert, it is often completely unimaginative. Vegans are as fed up with fruit salad and sorbet as vegetarians are with omelettes and cheese salad! Why not offer vegan ice cream (see above) with fruit salad, or better still, experiment with egg-free recipes for cakes and

puddings. It is possible to make delicious trifles, flans and cheesecakes which are completely vegan.

If you have any questions, or would like some free vegan cake recipes, write to me c/o Vegetarian Guides. You could also contact **the Vegan Society** (below) for their catering pack (which includes a list of wholesalers of vegan food and alcohol) and their merchandise catalogue full of cookbooks. Alternatively, see what's on offer in any of the restaurants listed that are particularly good for vegans. The IVU and VRG websites are also a great source of inspiration.

Ronny has been a vegan campaigner and caterer for many years, has written The Complete Scoffer *cookbook and co-authored* Campaign Against Cruelty – an activist's handbook. *She currently works as a campaigner at Animal Aid (www.animalaid.org.uk) and has published a vegan cookbook* **The Cake Scoffer,** *available by sending a cheque for £1.50 (£1 + 50p postage) to Animal Aid, The Old Chapel, Bradford St, Tonbridge, Kent TN9 1AW. www.animalaid.org.uk. Ronny's brand new* **The Salad Scoffer – picnic and party food recipes** *is £1.25 + 50p postage = £1.75 from Animal Aid (inflation y'know). See some Scoffer recipes at: www.campaignagainstcruelty.co.uk.*

Top websites for recipes & cookbooks:

International Vegetarian Union: www.ivu.org

The Vegetarian Society (UK): www.vegsoc.org
Parkdale, Dunham Rd, Altrincham, Cheshire WA14 4QG, UK
Tel (+44) 0161-925 2000, Fax 0161-926 9182. Email: info@vegsoc.org

Vegetarian Resource Group: www.vrg.org

The Vegan Society: www.vegansociety.com
Donald Watson House, 7 Battle Rd, St Leonards-on-Sea, East Sussex TN37 7AA, UK. Tel (+44) 0845 45 88244. Fax 01424-717064. Email: info@vegansociety.com
Profit From Emerging Dietary Trends: www.gopublish.co.uk

Animal-free cosmetics

What is cruelty free?

Against animal testing – this is practically worthless in our opinion. Probably they are using the ...

Five year rolling rule They don't use ingredients tested on animals in the last five years. So if it's force fed to animals today, they'd be happy to sell in five years. And of course the ingredients themselves could actually be made from animals, such as bath balls made from gelatine, or be made from egg or milk from (factory farmed) animals that have been raised for meat.

Fixed cut off date This means the company does not use any ingredients tested after a fixed date, such as 1984 or 1975. The earlier the better.

No animal ingredients Now we're talking. No animal parts, no milk, no eggs, no honey, no lanolin (made from wool), no insect parts.

Vegan If you see this, you can be sure there are no animal ingredients and it isn't bunny tested. Look out for the Vegan Society symbol.

In other words, look for no animal or animal derived ingredients (vegan) and a fixed cut off date for testing, the earlier the better. If the packaging carries the Vegan Society symbol then you can be assured that it will be as cruelty free as possible.

Läyne Kuirk-Schwarz-Waad has a degree in industrial chemistry and pharmacology and has a private practice as a natural health practitioner. (see page 261) She also teaches and writes for several health magazines. Here she tells us about her favourite products which are as cruelty free as possible, with no animal testing and no animal ingredients.

I have been a vegan for more than 21 years. I love all animals, especially if they happen to be rabbits. In both my personal and my professional life, I have always tried to support ethical businesses as a customer, employee and employer. For me, as a vegan and a Buddhist, cruelty free is absolutely essential, but not always easy to find. Lucky for me that I have an involvement with a couple of ethical natural health businesses, which enables me to check out just how free of cruelty (or not) manufacturers really are! Veggie Guides asked me to supply the low-down on some of the best health and body care to be found, so I have! Of course some wonderful people will be accidentally omitted I am sure, so if you think we have left somebody out – maybe it's you – get in touch with Alex and his merry little band and tell them all about it! After all, there's always the next edition! Anyway, here goes!

Dr Hauschka

Truly amazing and increasingly trendy array of therapeutic toiletries, supplements and cosmetics. Dr H are part of an ethical German organisation called Wala. You can see the famous Wala symbol on all the products and it represents their commitment to a respectful and harmonious relationship between humanity, animals, plants and minerals. All Wala members are bound by a code of ethical conduct, including no animal testing, no use of products that may have caused suffering to animals, organic/biodynamic farming methods, no use of products which may result in polluting the environment, no use of endangered plants, ethical employment principles, recycled and recyclable packaging.

Sadly, not everything is vegan. Some products contain

propolis wax, lanolin, beeswax, royal jelly or silk powder, but some of the range is being reformulated using vegan ingredients:

The following , I am delighted to tell you, are 100% animal-free (but check the label as ingredients may vary according to the country for which they were manufactured):

Cleansing Cream, Cleansing Milk, Facial Toner, Rose Day Cream and Quince Day Cream (hurrah they're now vegan, thank you rabbit goddess), Moisturising Day Cream, Normalising Day Oil, Eye Solace, Sensitive Rhythmic Conditioner, Clarifying Toner, Facial Steam Bath, Cleansing Clay Mask, Rejuvenating Mask, Inner Cosmetic Body Wash, Fresh Body Wash, Floral Bath Oils: lavender, lemon, rosemary, sage, spruce; Quince Body Moisturiser.

Body Oils: Birch & Arnica, Blackthorn, Lavender, Lemon, Moor Lavender, Rose (beautiful beyond belief!), Rosemary, St. John's Wort Neem Nail Oil, Rosemary Leg and Arm Toner, Fresh Deodorant and Floral Deodorant (now lanolin free), Fitness Leg Spray (excellent if you spend most of your day standing, for example on a Saturday outside a furrier's somewhere in the vicinity of Knightsbridge)

Pure Shampoo, Herbal Hair Conditioner, Neem Hair Oil, Neem Hair Lotion Eyeliner – all varieties, Mascara – all varieties, Lipliner – all varieties

Their UK distributor is Elysia, call them on 01386-792 622 for stockists near you. A wonderful Dr Hauschka therapist is Sally-Anne Sherfield, for treatments and gift vouchers 020-8543 9652.

Earth Mother

Sensitively and expertly handmade aromatherapy oils, body lotions, sprays, bath preparations and more, specially formulated for pregnancy, labour, post-natal, babies, children...and dads! All vegan, no animal testing, organic, recycled/biodegradable packaging, extremely pure and gentle. The range includes:

Arnica Gel (uses a water and xanthum gum base), Nappy Gel, Baby Massage Oil, Baby Bath, Children's Chest Rub (perfect for coughs & colds), Pregnancy Massage Oil, Perineum Massage Oil, Tummy Stretch Mark, Cream, New Body Lotion, Nipple Cream (needs no explanation, I hope!), Lavender Hydrolat Spray, Labour Massage Oil, New Father Body Splash etc.

Also, a lovely little collection of 'kits': Pregnancy Kit, Vegan Labour Kit (nothing to do with a certain Newham MP!), Childbirth Kit, Children's Care Kit.
If you would like more information, then contact Alan or Juliette on:020–8442 1704.

Green People

Registered with the Vegan Society, no animal testing, organic ingredients, pure, unfussy but sophisticated and they donate 10% of net profits to environmental charities which can't be bad. As everything Green People do is untainted by hoof, paw or any other part of an animal, I won't list all of their products, just a few to whet your appetite, but please don't eat them!

Gentle Cleanse, Gentle Tone, Fruit Scrub, Vita Min Mask (yes, I do know how to spell, this is just the name of the product), Day Solution, Fruitful Nights, Help at Hand, Eye Gel, Eye Cream, Gentle Body Polish, Aloe Vera Shampoo, Rosemary Shampoo, Vita Min Fix Shampoo, Aloe Vera Conditioner, Rosemary Conditioner, Vita Min Fix Conditioner, Hair Styling Gel, Aloe Vera Shower Gel, Rosemary & Pink Clay Shower Gel, Lavender & Rosemary Deodorant, Aloe Vera Deodorant.
Toothpastes (but watch out for new formulations with propolis from bees): Citrus, Mint, Fennel, Herbal & Mandarin (for kiddy-winkies); Mouthwashes, Sun Lotions.

Men's Care Range: no more excuses, boys! With Green People's revolutionary new range of vegan bodycare,

otherwise known as OrganicGuys.com, you can bathe again without fear – hoorah! Thank you Green People!
They also make some supplements, mainly herbs in Vegicaps. Customer Careline: 01444-401444, ask for Kay or Emily.

JÄSÖN

Apart from a couple of items containing honey, all of JÄSÖN's products are vegan. They also state that the use of animal experimentation is totally unacceptable to them and that they are prepared to go to great lengths not to pollute the environment, which seems to be convincingly backed-up by the fact that they are registered with the Humane Society of the U.S. and donate a percentage of their annual profits to animal, environmental and eco-active charities. All the packaging is recycled and recyclable and the contents biodegradable and organic when possible. The range is rather enormous, so I will list the darlings!

Beta-Gold Freshner, Quick Recovery Rehydrating Lotion, Meditation Masque, Vegee Tonic, Quick Clean Make-up Remover, Ultra-C Eye Lift, Woman Wise Wild Yam Cream (for those times in a woman's life when hormones just aren't fun anymore), Vitamin E Creme 25,000 i.u, 84% Aloe Vera, Natural Sea Kelp Shampoo, Henna Highlights Shampoo, Thin-to-Thick Body Building Hairspray; Apricot/Lavender/Tea Tree/Rose Satin Shower & Bubble Bath; Shaving Lotion for Beautiful Legs (nice, but don't expect miracles!), Sun Blocks, and more!

If you would like to seek out a stockist, call the UK distributor Kinetic Ltd on 020-7435 5911. (make sure you talk to someone who has all the latest info)

Urtekram

These people really do put their hearts and souls into what they do and, not surprisingly, the results are unbelievably good. All their products are made in their purpose-built wind and hay-powered factory in Denmark, are never tested on animals, are predominantly organic, biodegradable and almost entirely vegan, though the toothpastes contain propolis. Another great thing about this range is that a little does go a long way; the shampoos are triple concentrated and retail at around £2.99 for 250ml! Here's a selection of the loveliest:

Rose Shampoo, Rose Conditioner, Lavender Shampoo, Lavender Conditioner, Camomile Shampoo, Camomile Conditioner, Nettle Shampoo, Mud and Mint Shampoo, Children's Shampoo, Camomile Lotion, Rose Lotion, Lavender Lotion, Lavender Aftersun, Aloe Vera Soap, Rose Soap, Lavender Soap, Sandalwood Soap, Children's Soap, Tea Tree Soap.

To find out where to buy these fantastic things call Marigold Healthfoods, their major distributor in the UK on: 020-7388 4515.

BioCare

As for supplements, the cream of the crop, (that would be a soya or pea protein based cream, of course) has to be BioCare for me. Their formulations are ingenious to say the least, they are GM-free and offer an exceptional variety for vegetarians and vegans. They have an excellent technical support team who are always happy to answer your queries, whatever they might be. I shan't attempt to list every product suitable for veggies and vegans, so here is a taster of what is completely animal-free:

One-a-Day Multivitamins & Minerals, Vyta-Myn Formula, B Complex, Microcell Vitamin E, Magnesium Ascorbate (Vitamin C), Folguard (B12 & Folic Acid), Co Enzyme Q10 Plus, Zinc Citrate, Beetroot Complex (Iron Supplement), Evening Primrose Oil (in Vegcaps! Thank Goodness! Hell hath no fury like a pre-menstrual vegan woman, let me tell you!)

If you would like more information on retail outlets or mail order, then contact BioCare direct on:0121 433 3879

Läyne Kuirk-Schwarz-Waad can be contacted for a variety of treatments on 07985-120 101 or through the lovely VeggieGuides people at Layne@veggieguides.co.uk. See advert page 261.

Lush Shops in London

by Jennifer Wharton

Most Londoners can't have failed to see the brightly coloured Lush shops with their banana yellow fronts. Behind this vibrant facade lies a seriously committed veggie cosmetic company with a worldwide presence, probably only rivaled in scale by the, from a cruelty-free point of view, now defunct Body Shop. (Try asking which products are truly cruelty free – in other words vegan – on a Saturday and you'll see what we mean.)

With products created along clear vegetarian principles and 73% of these being suitable for vegans, Lush are certainly different from the rabbit torturing l'Oréals of this world, with fresh handmade cosmetics and toiletries. The only really annoying thing is that the vegan products aren't actually marked up in the shop, so you have to keep searching for them in the catalogue.

The Lush ethos is that the way you treat the outside of your body should be the same as the inside, so plenty of fresh fruit and veg and organic wherever possible. They aim to completely change the way people feel and act about cosmetics and their skin.

Pick up a Lush newspaper-style catalogue in one of the shops for the lowdown on the latest products, skin care advice, tips and reviews from members of the public. It's really humor-ously written so you can have a laugh at the same time. Find them in London at the following addresses:

123 Kings Road, London SW3 4PL
Unit 11, The Piazza, Covent Garden, London WC2E 8RA
40 Carnaby Street, London W1V 1PD
27 Market Place, Kingston-upon-Thames KT1 1JH
There are around another 18 stores throughout Britain and Ireland.

ARE YOU FED UP WITH CRUELTY TO ANIMALS?

THEN GIVE US A HAND!

If you are opposed to the many forms of animal abuse in London - the meat trade, fur shops, animal experiments, etc - then join London Animal Action and campaign for an end to such cruelties.

We have been actively campaigning since 1991 by organising protests and demonstrations, and we hold meetings on the second Monday of each month at Marchmont Community Centre, 62 Marchmont St, London WC1, at 7:30pm. Nearest tube: Russell Square. Delicious vegan refreshments available.

Our main campaign in recent years has been against the London fur trade. As a direct pressure from activists, two major fur shops in central London closed down in 1999.

We also organise transport to demos outside London, for example against Huntingdon Life Sciences.

We publish a regular newsletter, London Animal Rights News, which you can receive for one year by sending a cheque for at least £5 (3£ unwaged) payable to "LAA" to:

London Animal Action, BM 2248, London WC1N 3XX.
Phone: 0845 4584775 email: laa@londonaa.demon.co.uk
Website: www.londonaa.demon.co.uk

Get active !
Local groups

Some of these are campaigning groups – these usually have the word "animal". Others are mainly social – look for the word "vegan" or "vegetarian".

Animal Alliance (Enfield)

PO Box 194, Enfield, Middlesex EN1 3HD.

Animal Defence League

PO Box 5041, Theydon Bois, Epping, Essex CM16 7DG.
Website: http://www.liberation-mag.freeserve.co.uk/

Asian Vegan and Vegetarian Association

Mobile 07950-665547

Barnet Animal Rights

PO Box 76, Barnet, Herts EN4 9AW   *Tel: 020-8446 3480*
Email: barg@bmjjhr.easynet.co.uk

Bromley Animal Rights

16 Parkside Avenue, Bromley BR1 2EJ   *Tel: 020-8464 6035*

Bromley and Environs Vegetarian Group

For the latest newsletter send
9 x inch sae to Kathy Silk, BEVEG, c/o Bronwen Humphreys, The Vegetarian Society, Parkdale, Dunham Rd, Altrincham, Cheshire WA14 4QG.

Campaign Against Leather & Fur

BM Box 8880, London WC1N 3XX
www.veganfestival.freeserve.co.uk

Organisers of annual National Vegan Festival in Summer.

Campaign in London for Animal Welfare (CLAW)

PO Box 14513, London, N22 6WB.   *Tel: 020-8888 4971*

Croydon Vegans & Vegetarians

pat_croydon_vegans@hotmail.com   *Tel: 020-8654 3740.*
http://uk.geocities.com/croydon_vegans
croydon_vegans@yahoo.co.uk

We organise and stage local campaigning events, both in conjunction with Animal Aid and with other like-minded organisations. Volunteers are always welcome and should get in touch with Pat either by e-mail or by telephone.

Croydon Vegetarians

Helen Buckland   *Tel: 020-8688 6325*

East London Animal Rights

PO Box 216, Forest Gate, London E7 9RB.   *Tel 020-8555 6683*

Elmbridge Animal Aid
and Compassion in World Farming

local contact for SW London Elizabeth Shaw   *Tel: 020-8398 4003*

Gay Vegetarians and Vegans

GV, BM 5700, London WC1N 3XX

Kingston and Richmond Vegetarians

Martin 020–8541 3437, John 020–8977 9648

Kingston Stop Animal Suffering

37 Arlington Rd, Surbiton, Surrey KT6 6BW.

Leaves of Life

The Advent Centre, Banqueting Suite   *Tel: 020–8881 8865*
39 Brendon Street, London W1
(Corner of Crawford Place and Brendon Street)
e-mail leavesoflife@aol.com

This vegan organisation meets usually once a month at the above address. They promote the health aspects of vegan nutrition. A typical meeting starts with a cookery demonstration followed by a lecture by a vegan doctor or health practitioner. Topics include diabetes, osteoporosis, hydrotherapy, cancer, arthritis, ulcers, digestive orders, atherosclerosis and how a plant based diet avoids or helps reverse these. For more details phone or e-mail.

London Animal Action

BM 2248, London WC1N 3XX   *Tel / Fax:*
meeting address: Marchmont Community Centre,   *0845-458 4775*
62 Marchmont Street, London WC1.   *(local rate)*
Tube: Russell Square (Piccadilly Line, closest),
Chancery Lane, Euston, King's Cross, Euston Square.
Bus 7, 59, 68, 91, 168
www.londonaa.demon.co.uk, larn@londonaa.demon.co.uk

Meetings: 7.30–9.00pm, 2nd Monday of the month. Vegan food served afterwards. Extremely active campaigning group with weekly anti-fur demos in London, minibuses to animal abusing establishments around the country, street stalls, monthly newsletter.

South London Animal Action

PO Box 594, London. SW9 8QG   Tel: 020-8293 9796

London Vegans

7 Deansbrook Road, Edgware, Middlesex. HA8 9BE   Zena 020-7354 8256,
meetings: Millman Street Community Rooms,   Paul 01206-861846.
Millman St, London. WC1.   Infoline: 020-8931 1904
Email: londonvegans@onet.co.uk
www.londonvegans.freeserve.co.uk

Meetings: 6.30pm, last Wednesday of the month (not December), east of
Russell Square underground, entrance through security doors adjacent to
38a, press the bell marked Community Centre.

RAWFARE

Karen, North Finchley   Tel: 020-8446 2960
karen@rawfare.freeserve.co.uk

Information on the raw food lifestyle, natural diet and wholefood
philosophy. Books and meetings. Affiliated to FRESH and Nature's First
Law (see www.rawfood.com). www.fresh-network.com for heaps of links
to raw food things. A Rawfare website is on the way.

G, High Barnet   Tel: 020-8441 6252

SJ Lewis and friends, raw food caterers   Tel: 020-7729 4233

Ivor, Juice Bar catering   Tel: 020-8544 9494

Jill Swyers, SW8, teacher of nutrition at Regents Park   Tel: 020-8870 7041
College of Naturopathic Medicine,info@jillswyers.com.

Muslim Vegan and Vegetarian Society

Rafeeque Ahmed, 59 Brey Towers, 136 Adelaide   *Tel: 020-7483 1742.*
Road, London NW3 3JU.

Publishes Islam and Vegetarianism book, for £1 post free. Main emphasis is on the vegan side, also raw food, combining, timing and additive free.

Vegan World Ventures

Info from Ahsan   *Tel: 020-8220 2003.*

Outdoor activities, camping, cycling, hiking around London. Free of charge

Vegetarian Cycling and Athletic Club

Running, Peter Simpson 01908-503919
Cycling, Nick Guy 0116-259 3754
Triathlon, Steve Coote 01582-666243

Vegetarian Social Club

Helen Buckland   *Tel: 020-8688 6325*

Veggies Nosh

Lisa Ceneri   *Tel: 01992-308319*

Waltham Cross. Monthly meetings, £5 donation appreciated

Walthamstow Animal Rights

PO Box 2344, London E17 6QR

Young Indian Vegetarians

Nitin Mehta, M.B.E., 226 London Rd,   *Tel: 020-8681 8884*
West Croydon, Surrey CR0 2TE

Organise annual rally and picnic in Hyde Park.

HUNT SABOTEURS

Hunt Saboteurs Association, PO Box 2786,   *Tel: 01273-622827*
Brighton BN2 2AX.

Fancy a different day out in the country while Tony Blair vacillates about implementing laws passed with a landslide years ago? Contact your local hunt sabs and join the national association. If you don't want to risk getting beaten up by hunters and terriermen while the police stand by, you can always help with street stalls and fund raising.

For a comprehensive national list of hunt saboteur groups, visit the Hunt Saboteurs Association website www.huntsabs.org.uk. Email: hsa@gn.apc.org. For national news on hunt sabotage, join the HSA and receive their quarterly magazine, HOWL. Membership is £10 a year.

Brixton Hunt Saboteurs
121 Railton Rd, London SE24 0LR

Croydon Hunt Saboteurs   *Tel: 07956-359 891*
PO Box 1072, Coulsdon, Surrey CR5 2ZT

North London Hunt Saboteurs
PO Box 11327, London N1 0XQ.

South Essex Hunt Saboteurs
PO Box 135, Basildon, Essex, SS15 5SA.

West London Hunt Saboteurs   *Tel: 020-7278 3068.*
c/o LAA, BM 2248, London WC1N 3XX.

East London Hunt Saboteurs   *Tel: 020-8534 1326.*
PO Box 571, Brentwood, Essex CM14 4AA.

London Hunt Saboteurs Hot-line   *Tel: 01895-813339*

THE NATIONALS

If there's no vegetarian or animal rights group listed near you, contact any of these for the address of your local contact or group. If you want to go veggie or vegan, or know someone who might be interested, they have stacks of literature to help you and can answer questions. If you want to help spread the word and get active for animal rights, they would love to hear from you. And they all have brilliant websites. Always enclose a stamped addressed envelope.

Animal Aid

The Old Chapel, Bradford St, Tonbridge,
Kent TN9 1AW.
www.animalaid.org.uk

Tel: 01732-364 546.
Fax: 01732-366 533.

£10 waged, £7 unwaged, £5 youth. The experts on U-18 campaigns for all areas of animal rights including vivisection, school dissection, school debates, displays, vegetarianism, veganism, circuses, zoos. See page 59.

The Vegan Society

7 Battle Rd, St Leonards-on-Sea,
East Sussex TN37 7AA.
www.vegansociety.com

Tel: 0845-4588244
Fax 01424-717064

£21 sub, £14 low income. Publishes The Vegan magazine, The Animal Free Shopper book, Vegan Nutrition, the video Truth or Dairy, 70 information sheets which are also on line. Send £1 stamps or cheque for their 16 page introductory booklet Go Vegan. Merchandise catalogue includes all the books you'll need to be a happy, healthy, deliciously fed vegan.

The Vegetarian Society

Parkdale, Dunham Rd, Altrincham,
Cheshire WA14 4QG.
www.vegsoc.org

Tel: 0161-925 2000.
Fax: 0161-926 9182.

£21, £16 unwaged, £8 U-16, brings you four copies of The Vegetarian magazine and access to their helpline. Huge network of local groups and contacts. Organises National Vegetarian Week in May. See page 8.

Veggies, Nottingham

www.veggies.org.uk   Tel: 0845-458 9595

Publishes the Animal Rights Calendar and Animal Contacts Directory, available on line, which lists every veggie and vegan business and animal rights group in the country.

Viva! (Vegetarians International Voice for Animals)

12 Queen Square, Brighton BN1 3FD   Tel: 01273-777 688.
www.viva.org.uk   Fax: 01273-776 755.

Everything for the new veggie or vegan or the established one who wants to convert all her friends and family. The most comprehensive book catalogue in the movement plus tons for kids. Speakers for school talks.

Animal Rights Coalition

PO Box 339 , Wolverhampton WV10 7BZ.   Tel: 0845-458 0146

www.arcnews.co.uk, www.betrayed.co.uk
and www.realfood.org.uk

Network of Britain's 500 most active local animal rights groups and grass-roots campaigners. For local animal rights news from around the country, subscribe to 12 monthly issues of ARCNews newsletter for £10. Booklet Veganism – the way forward for £1.

People for the Ethical Treatment of Animals

PETA Europe Ltd, PO Box 36668, London SE1 1WA   Tel: 020 7357 9229
E: info@petauk.org   Fax: 020 7357 0901
www.PETAUK.org

The biggest animal rights campaigning organisation in the world. Free Vegetarian Starter Kits are always available from their homepage. See also page 13.

London Vegans

We meet for a talk or video on the last Wednesday evening of the month (except December) in central London. Come and join us for a discussion, a snack, and pick up some leaflets and a free copy of the London Vegans What's On Diary. From 18.30 till 21.00 we'll be at Millman Street Community Rooms, 52 Millman St, WC1, east of Russell Square underground. Entrance through security doors next to 38a, press the bell marked Community Centre then go all the way round the building and down. Afterwards some of us go on to the local pub.

We organise many social events such as restaurant and pub evenings, walks and outings, and also go out campaigning, with information stalls throughout the year. We meet many of our friends through London Vegans and so could you.

Send sae for more details, or become a member now for just £3.00 by post or £2.00 by email and receive regular copies of our comprehensive guide to veggie events in London for one year.

London Vegans, 7 Deansbrook Road, Edgware,
Middlesex. HA8 9BE.

Or contact Zena 020-7354 8256, Paul 01206-861846.
24-hour infoline: 020-8931 1904.

www.londonvegans.freeserve.co.uk
Email: londonvegans@onet.co.uk

Getting away

"One of the simplest and most powerful ways to rekindle passion is to get out of the house on a romantic getaway.... Try to get away at least one night a month."

John Gray, *Mars And Venus In The Bedroom*

Romantic dinners, birthday and anniversary celebrations don't have to be limited to London. Or even Britain. It's now cheaper to fly to Europe than to go by train to some parts of Britain. Try www.ryanair.com, easyjet.com and go-fly.com. Here are ideas for a weekend break with great veggie grub.

BRIGHTON

The ideal day out from London, get the train from Victoria station. The area around the Laines is packed with lovely little shops, veggie cafés and even a veggie pub. Don't miss Vegetarian Shoes in Gardner Street (closed Sundays). For places to stay, check out the big Brighton section in **Vegetarian Britain** or invest in a copy of **Vegetarian Brighton**.

EDINBURGH

With many central veggie restaurants, a castle, heaps of nightlife and shopping, this is an essential weekend away. Cheap flights from City or Stanstead airport, try Ryan Air, Easyjet or British Midland. Or do a sleeper on the train. Our favourite place to stay out of several options in *Vegetarian Britain* and *Vegetarian Europe* is the amazingly friendly Greenhouse vegetarian guest-house, complete with an awesome full Scottish cooked veggie breakfast, even vegan soaps and bedding.

PARIS

The ultimate romantic weekend, only three hours by Eurostar from Waterloo station, with fares from £70 if you book at least two weeks ahead and no airport hassles. You'll find 20 veggie restaurants in the Paris section of *Vegetarian Europe*, mostly tucked away in side streets. (If you still have the first edition of *Vegetarian France*, note that Country Life and La Truffe restaurants have closed.) Although the standards are not yet as high as in London, you'll still be spoilt for choice. Paris is especially good if you like macrobiotic food.

AMSTERDAM

Amsterdam is particularly popular with younger veggies with its cheap, party atmosphere hostels, no language barrier so it's easy to make friends, and an enlightened lack of formality or rules for rules' sake. Highlights are strolling through the canals, all-you-can-eat falafel stalls, the hilarious Sex Museum, the Hemp Museum, markets, bars and coffee shops with particularly relaxing coffee. And lots of veggie eateries listed in *Vegetarian Europe*.

DUBLIN

Apart from veggie cafés in, you've guessed it, *Vegetarian Europe*, this young, fashionable trendy capital is very popular for weekends away, hen and stag nights, for example at Bono and the Edge's nightclub the Grafton on the river Liffey, close to the Temple Bar area where young folks go to party and dance away Friday and Saturday night. Everything is within walking distance including some very nice shops.

BARCELONA

Home of Modernism with a park dedicated to Gaudi, the

whole city is an eclectic mix of architecture and history. Tons of bars and cafés, especially in the Barrigotic area where you can get great veggie grub like falafels, hummous and Indian dishes. It's also good for kids with a funicular railway up to a massive funfair on top of a hill overlooking the city and the sea. The Olympic village is pretty amazing too. Great eateries are listed in **Vegetarian Europe** or the brand new **Vegetarian Spain**.

PRAGUE

Dominated by the hilltop castle, Prague offers delightful sightseeing with quaint old squares, warm sunshine and the slinkiest local accents in Europe. With plenty of cheap hostels, it's a party town and magnet for backpackers. And there are two great veggie restaurants right in the middle.

We could go on, and on, about Copenhagen, Venice, Florence, Rome, Brussels and forty more European or dozens of British cities. Instead we'll say just get yourself a copy of **Vegetarian Europe** or **Vegetarian Europe** from any UK or American bookstore or mail order from us, and start dreaming. Other guides available mail order from us.

NEW YORK

The greatest concentration of veggie and vegan eateries outside London, unbelievable shopping, gorgeous accents, terrific shows, movies that haven't even been released here and the lowest airfares ever. The food is in **The Vegan Guide to New York City** available mail order from Veggie Guides.

Do you get the impression that this whole section is just one big advertisement? Well yes it is. For veggie fun, adventure, romance, excitement and cosmopolitan dining around the world.

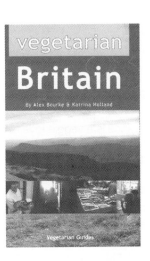

VEGETARIAN
FRANCE

edited by Alex Bourke and Alan Todd, with an
introduction by Roselyne Masselin of La Cuisine Imaginaire.

"A lot of people think it's impossible to find vegetarian food in France, but this little cracker of a book proves them wrong. Vegetarian France is an invaluable guide to finding really good vegetarian food in the most unexpected places. Bon appetit!"
Paul and Linda McCartney

France is a veggie-lover's paradise, but only if you know where to find it! This *128 page* guide features:

150 places to eat out and crash out, over **20** veggie restaurants in Paris alone, vegetarian hotels and guest houses all over France, all-you-can-eat vegan buffet in Marseille, veggie vocabulary, maps, the hitch-hiker's guide to the south of France on 50 francs a day, connect with fellow veggies in France!

Vegetarian Guides

Available from UK bookshops, price £6.99

VEGAN GUIDE TO
NEW YORK

by Rynn Berry & Chris A. Suzuki with Barry Litsky. 8th edition revised and updated. From Harlem to Wall Street, Manhattan is vegan and veggie nirvana with over 100 restaurants plus health food stores, ethnic cuisine, famer's markets, bookstores, even where to buy vegan shoes. Handy map of the favorite 22 NYC eating places. Also includes Queen's and Brooklyn.

The Vegan Guide

To

NEW YORK CITY

By

RYNN BERRY &
CHRIS A. SUZUKI

With Barry Litsky, J.D.

8th Edition
Revised &
Updated

Over 100 Restaurants • Health Food • Ethnic Cuisine

£6.99 + postage from Vegetarian Guides
Also available in USA from the publisher $9.95 + $1.50 postage to Rynn Berry, 159 Eastern Parkway, Suite 2H, Brooklyn, NY 11238

Campaign Against Cruelty

an animal activist's handbook

by Alex Bourke and Ronny Worsey

We tell you how to:

launch a local campaigning **group**
*run different kinds of **street stalls***
arrange a meeting or video showing
speak in public or to groups
produce **leaflets, posters and
newsletters**
raise money
promote veggie and vegan food in
your area
organise a demonstration
utilise the **press, radio and tv**
*understand how **the law** affects your
right to protest*
192 pages

£4.99 from UK and USA bookshops

Plus a huge **directory of books, magazines, websites and groups** that can provide you with info on all aspects of campaigning.

Relied on by group founders throughout the country and written by two dedicated, effective and inspiring campaigners, with contributions from frontline activists throughout Britain and overseas, this book contains all the advice you need to start saving animals' lives now.

So, what are you waiting for?

The entire book online at **www.CampaignAgainstCruelty.co.uk**

VEGAN PASSPORT

edited by George Rodger of the Vegan Society

We've all been in a foreign restaurant and explained to the waiter in basic English what we want, only for the cook to serve up soup with a bone at the bottom or salad with tuna. Not any more! This passport sized book contains a page for each of the 38 most common languages covering 90% of the world's population, saying what vegans do and don't eat in great detail.

Let the waiter show it to the cook and you'll be sure of a totally animal free feast even if no one speaks a word of your language. Includes all of the European Community, Arabic, Bengali, Chinese, Croatian, Czech, Gujarati, Hebrew, Hindi, Hungarian, Indonesian, Japanese, Korean, Malay, Marathi, Persian, Polish, Romanian, Russian, Sinhalese, Slovak, Swahili, Tagalog, Thai, Turkish, Urdu, Vietnamese and Esperanto. Plus a page of pictures of what we do and don't eat if all else fails.

The essential companion to *Vegetarian Europe*.

£2.99 + postage from Vegetarian Guides

VEGETARIAN GUIDES
mapping the world for vegetarians and vegans

Our own guides, available from bookshops:
BRITAIN £7.95, EUROPE £9.99, FRANCE £6.99, LONDON £5.99
CAMPAIGN AGAINST CRUELTY £4.99
All other guides we buy in and are available *mail order only.*
BRIGHTON £2.99, NY CITY £6.99, ITALY £6.99, ISRAEL £6.99
SPAIN £6.99, VEGAN PASSPORT £2.99, ANIMAL FREE SHOPPER £4.99
CAKE SCOFFER £1, RAINBOWS & WELLIES £14.95, ANIMAL RIGHTS video £9.95

Please send me:
[ ] *Vegetarian Britain* £7.95
[ ] *Europe* £9.99   [ ] *Israel* £6.99
[ ] *France* £6.99   [ ] *NY City* £6.99
[ ] *London* £5.99   [ ] *Brighton* £2.99
[ ] *Spain* £7.99   [ ] *Cake Scoffer* £1
[ ] *Italy* £6.99   [ ] *Passport* £2.99
[ ] *Campaign Against Cruelty* £4.99
[ ] *Animal Rights* video £9.95
[ ] *Animal Free Shopper* £4.99
[ ] *Rainbows & Wellies* cookbook £14.95

Postage & packing rates:
UK one book £1.50, then £1 per book.
[ ] Airmail to Europe, surface other countries, £2.25 then £1.50 per book.
[ ] Airmail to rest of world one book £3 then £2 per book.

Money back guarantee: if for any reason you are not entirely satisfied, return within 28 days for a full, no quibble refund. This guarantee is in addition to your statutory rights.

Sub total £ . . . . . plus p&p £ . . . . . .   TOTAL £ . . . . . .
[ ] I enclose a UK sterling cheque/PO/money order payable to 'Vegetarian Guides Ltd'
[ ] Please debit my Visa/Mastercard/Access/Eurocard/Visa Delta/Connect/Switch/Solo

Card number . . . .   Start date . . . . . Expiry . . . .

Switch Issue No . . . Name on card . . . .

Name: . . . .   Telephone: . . . .

Address: . . . .

. . . .   Postcode . . . .

Email: . . . .   Today's date: . . . .

Signature . . . .

Mail to: Vegetarian Guides Ltd, PO Box 2284, London W1A 5UH, England.
Or fax to (outside UK +44) 0870-121 4721. USA fax: +1-509-272 1463.
Order online at www.vegetarianguides.com,
enquiries: info@vegetarianguides.com

For the latest updates to this book
and other Veggie Guides, visit

www.vegetarianguides.co.uk

All over London
Indexes

Restaurants

A

B

C

H

I

J

K

L

M

V

W

Y

Shops

F

G

H

J

L

M

N

O

P

Q

R

S

T

V

W

All you can eat buffets